A Tragedy Waiting to Happen

The Chaotic Life of
BRENDAN O'DONNELL

TONY AND JJ MUGGIVAN

Gill & Macmillan

Gill & Macmillan Ltd
Hume Avenue
Park West
Dublin 12
with associated companies throughout the world
www.gillmacmillan.ie

© 2004 Tony and JJ Muggivan

0 7171 3784 8

Print origination by
Carrigboy Typesetting Services, Co. Cork
Printed by AIT Nørhaven A/S, Denmark

*The paper used in this book is made from the wood pulp of managed
forests. For every tree felled, at least one tree is planted,
thereby renewing natural resources.*

A catalogue record is available for this book from the British Library.

1 3 5 4 2

For permission to reproduce photographs the authors and publisher
gratefully acknowledge the following: Press 22: pp 1 (both), 2, 3, 4
(both), 6 (top right), 7 (bottom); John Kelly at *The Clare Champion*:
pp 5 (both), 6 (top left & bottom), 7 (top)

Contents

CONTENTS

Acknowledgments

Thanks to Dermot and Ann O'Sullivan, Michael O'Sullivan, Joe and Vera O'Rourke, Carmel Burke, Tony and Josephine O'Brien, Ann Marie O'Donnell, Mrs Quinn, Tom and B. Mae Dinan, Frank Muggivan, Ann and Stephen O'Farrell, John and Maisie O'Rourke, Norbert and Helga Hau, Patricia Donnellan, Edward Corry, Liam and Theresa Flannery, Frank McDermot, Joe Duffy, Dennis Woods and Rose Tiernan.

Dedicated to my wife, Mary, and sons Brendan, Kevin, Gerard and Ross, and daughter-in-law, Erin

Tony

Thanks to Alyson Mitchell, Devi Subramaniam, Joyce Whetstone, Maria Shcherbakov, Dale Hickey, Margie Miller, Susan Parisi, Cheryl Roche, Angela Reid, Angela Amato and Kate Kane Laborde for much appreciated encouragement, advice and support. Bridget Jatho, Christy McGrail Ferguson, Sean Muggivan and Patti Muggivan for very valuable editing. Mary Ann McGrath Swaim for her valuable insights on food obsession, and Jirina Fiala for hours of consultation and readiness to listen. A special thanks to the entire Irish community in New Orleans and my colleagues and staff at the Center for Individual and Family Counseling, who have wondered if this story would ever reach print. My gratitude to the staff of Gill & Macmillan for their help in the final stages of preparation.

Dedicated to my wife, Patti; to my son, Sean; to my daughter, Joni

JJ

Introduction

Tony Muggivan

———————

Today, the first day of November 2002, I visited the Clonrush graveyard in Whitegate. For Catholics, 1 November, the day after Halloween, is a day for visiting the graves to pray for their dead relatives. The day is called 'All Souls' Day'.

I went to the graveyard particularly to remember Brendan O'Donnell and his mother, Margaret. As I was driving there, I remembered accounts of Brendan's visits after his mother died and of his urgent requests to his sister to visit her grave when he was in prison and couldn't make the trip himself. I wondered if Brendan had ever been able to believe or imagine his mother at rest.

My own family graveyard is on an island in Lough Derg, an island about two miles by boat from the village of Mountshannon. This island is commonly called 'Holy Island' or Iniscealtra. It has ruins of seven old churches dating back to before the time of the Vikings. It has an unfinished round tower, built as a place of safety for the monks during Viking raids on the island's monastery.

We usually don't visit this graveyard on All Souls' Day. At this time of the year, the weather can be cold and wet, and nearly all of the boats used on the lake are open boats.

Clonrush graveyard is on the mainland. It is located a couple of hundred yards from the western shore of Lough Derg and faces across the lake towards County Tipperary.

Only the mother was buried. Brendan's ashes — actually only half of his ashes — were scattered on top of his mother's grave. After he had been cremated, his ashes were divided between his father, Michael Pat, and his sister, Ann Marie. His father scattered his half of the ashes on Brendan's mother's grave.

I haven't been able to let go of my memories of Brendan O'Donnell and the memories of his time in my home. They are deeply embedded in my mind. I can never forget the killings and those awful days at the end of April and beginning of May in 1994.

As I walked up to the grave, I saw an elderly man standing there. When I got closer, I saw that the headstone had been smashed into pieces, obviously smashed with a sledgehammer. The man standing at the grave looked upset at the sight in front of him. I recognised him as Brendan's uncle.

I cursed and said to him, 'Who would do something like this? They must be very sick.' He said that the family would have the headstone repaired.

I walked away and thought to myself that cursing wasn't much good. I spoke to a few people at a grave nearby and asked them what they thought had happened. One person said, lamely, that it must have been the wind. It was the only broken headstone in the graveyard.

I thought of another grave in the churchyard in Mountshannon where the bodies of parish priests are buried. There are four priests buried there — three former parish priests and one priest who was never a priest in our parish. He was a native of Mountshannon village who had worked for years in England.

One Sunday as I was going into Mass, past the priests' graves, I saw that the top half of one of the headstones was missing. The headstone, like the other three headstones, had been a cross about three feet tall. The top of the cross had been cut off, about halfway up the upright beam, by someone using a masonry saw. There was nothing left but the base and a short, ugly stump sticking up out of it.

The base had the priest's name on it and a brief legend about his life. The priest and Brendan were acquainted with each other.

Brendan, in his short life, suffered much pain and he inflicted much pain. I don't know if the priest suffered pain but I do know that he left his Church harmed and he left many of his parishioners angry and disillusioned. I recall confronting another parish priest, a very kindly man, about the priest's reputation with children. He cried and tearfully said, 'I thought he had overcome his problems years ago.'

As I drove home from my All Souls' Day visit to Clonrush graveyard, I couldn't stop thinking about all that has happened in my life over the past thirteen years. I recalled again how many people have suffered so much when it all might have been avoided.

Tony Muggivan

1

First Encounter

Tony Muggivan

I first got to know Brendan O'Donnell on a cold February night in 1989. I have read all the newspaper stories, watched all the television stories, and I attended much of his trial in 1996. I have been interviewed myself many times and tried to tell his story. I am so tired of never seeing the story of what really happened.

I have tried to tell it to people I hoped would record what happened. But as the years have gone by, I have recognised that I must tell the story myself. It has not left my mind, and maybe telling it will help me to leave it behind.

I need to introduce myself and my family, or at least the members of my family who were involved with me, one way or another, in the life of Brendan O'Donnell. My wife's name is Mary and I have four sons. At the time I first met Brendan, an elderly aunt and my wife's sister, Vera O'Sullivan, were living with us at our home. Our home is a farmhouse in Derrycon.

Derrycon is a townland ranging from a mile to two miles west-northwest of Mountshannon and overlooking Lough Derg, a lake on the River Shannon. Mountshannon is a village close to the shore of Lough Derg. It is about midway up the Clare side of the lake, between Killaloe and Portumna.

Killaloe is a town in Clare on the south end of Lough Derg, and Portumna is a town in Galway about thirty-five miles north on the other end of the lake.

At weekends, two of my wife's brothers would visit us from where they worked in Shannon Airport. We often had a full house. However, we own a fairly large farm-house so there was always plenty of room for everyone.

The year was 1989 and the time of the year was mid-February. To be exact it was Thursday night, 16 February 1989. The weather was very cold, as it usually is at that time of the year.

It was about 10.30 on a very wet night. There was a mixture of snow, sleet and rain falling. We had a big fire in the fireplace. And we needed a big fire. We were all watching a movie on TV.

We were very comfortable when the dog, a German Shepherd named Tiger, began to bark outside. For the dog to bark at this time of the night was unusual. We live about a mile from the village of Mountshannon, and about a quarter of a mile in off the road that passes our house. This road has very little traffic, especially at night.

Brendan, my oldest son, went out to see what was wrong and to see if some cattle had moved. I was watching the movie and didn't pay much attention.

After a few minutes, my son came back inside and said to me, 'Give me the keys to the car.' I found this strange and I asked him what for.

He said he wanted to go a short distance up the road and he said, 'Trust me.'

I looked at him for a second and decided to give them to him. He was about fifteen years old at the time.

After about a quarter of an hour, he came back and told me that Brendan O'Donnell was outside. I had heard of Brendan O'Donnell. I knew that he had been due back in Trinity House detention centre in Dublin over a week before, and I had heard the reports that he had absconded. But I had never seen him before in my life.

I told my son to bring him in. He was gone for what seemed like ten minutes, and he told me later that he was trying to convince the boy to come inside.

When my son came back, bringing the other Brendan with him, I couldn't believe what I saw. He was shivering with the cold, with mud up to his knees, soaking wet through and through, looking like a bullock or a cow that had just been pulled from a bog hole.

He was very nervous.

Mary started getting some of our son's clothes — our son, Brendan, was about the same age and size — while Vera began to cook some food for him. He said that he hadn't eaten for days, that he was on the run from the guards, and that he was not going back to prison, no matter what. He took a bath and changed his clothes.

After he had had some food, we talked up to about two o'clock in the morning. He told us about his mother's illnesses, her attempts to commit suicide, her death, and her burial. He told us that he had believed for a while that she was buried alive, locked inside her coffin, not able to get out.

He made me promise I wouldn't call the guards to report him. Mary prepared a bed for him and we all turned in for the night.

Next morning, I got up early and did the farm work as soon as I could. I told my wife that I was going to drive around to see if there were any guards in the neighbourhood conducting a search. I talked to different people I met, trying to get an exact story about what was being reported regarding Brendan. I met one garda car but it didn't appear to be going anywhere in particular.

I returned home, and as I was having a cup of tea and something to eat, I had a chat with my wife about what we were doing. We were protecting a young lad whom the courts had sent to prison. Could we be up on charges? We had to find a way to get him back into the judicial system.

We decided to tell the guards that the boy was in the forest near our house but wouldn't come out unless they would promise not to send him back to Trinity House. Now, we had to convince Brendan that this was the only way to help him. This was really hard to do with the condition he was in.

I got in contact with my brother, JJ, in New Orleans, to get advice from him. He is a social worker who in the course of his career has worked with a lot of troubled youngsters.

He told me to try to get him as much help as possible from the state as I couldn't hide or keep him forever. Brendan was very distrustful and it took a long time to convince him that this was the only thing to do.

On another dark, wet evening, two days later, I dropped him off at the edge of the forest and told him I would go and talk to Garda O'Hara in Mountshannon. The plan was that I would come back with the guard and arrange for the two to talk.

I spoke to Garda O'Hara and he agreed to come with me as I had proposed. Brendan had already told me that he knew Garda O'Hara, but at this time I didn't know they had a long history with each other.

When I came back with the guard, Brendan refused to come out of the forest, and an argument started. He told the guard he would never go back to Trinity House. He said, 'You don't know what it's fucking like — the fucking cunts can do what they like with you.' He said he would kill himself before he would go back.

It seemed to take a long time to get his confidence and we had to promise him that we would help him in every way. I promised that I would drive to Trinity House and find out for myself what was going on.

All three of us came back to my house. Garda O'Hara remarked, suspiciously, on how dry and clean Brendan's clothes were. In order to protect me, Brendan said he had been staying in an old outhouse in Whitegate. On this point, the guard didn't seem to believe either Brendan or myself.

We talked for several hours. Then Brendan told us where he had hidden his bag of clothes. The guard and I drove to get them. It was about four miles away. Because it was now late and dark, we brought flashlights with us.

My God! When I saw the old stable, with all the holes in the roof, I couldn't believe he had lived a week in a place like this — and in the weather we had been having.

I continued to phone my brother in New Orleans. He had a friend named Joe Carney who now worked in Ballinasloe Hospital. Ballinasloe is in County Galway and is about thirty miles from my house. Joe Carney and my brother attended university together in New Orleans and were in the same line of work. My brother advised me to contact Joe as he would be familiar with how to get help for someone like Brendan in Ireland.

Joe came as soon as I called him. After he had talked to Brendan for some time, he told me that he belonged in a mental hospital and that I should get him into one as soon as possible. Joe also talked to Garda O'Hara who was keeping his superintendent informed on what was happening.

We all agreed that we would take Brendan to a doctor and get a week's medical extension in order to avoid his having to return to Trinity House immediately. We did this on Saturday and got the extension.

We agreed to use the week to try to get him into a mental hospital. He was in a very bad condition and was suicidal. Joe Carney told us that being suicidal made his situation critical.

On Tuesday, 21 February, I took him back to the doctor. The doctor made some enquiries about getting him into Our Lady's Mental Hospital in Ennis, County Clare, but couldn't get him in there. I heard later from P.J. Flannery, a member of staff from Mountshannon, that a decision had been made to have nothing to do with Brendan, but that this decision did not have the backing of all the staff. P.J., a mental-health nurse, was disappointed with it, as was at least one of the doctors.

On Joe Carney's advice, I decided to try St Bridget's Hospital. Next morning, Mary and I had a long talk; we saw this as our only chance to get help for Brendan. We were hopeful that Joe Carney would be able to help him if he were hospitalised at St Bridget's.

I had very little cash at the time, and we are not very well off, even in the best of times. The cows hadn't started calving yet and we had no milk to sell to the creamery. However, I did have eleven hundred pounds and Mary and I decided to offer it to Ballinasloe Hospital as an incentive to help him. Deciding to leave ourselves short of money, if need be, we started for Ballinasloe the following morning.

I told Brendan that I would try my best to get him whatever help I could, and he seemed ready enough to do what I asked him to do.

On the way to Ballinasloe, he became very, very agitated. I told him I had enough money to get him started with counselling and that I was not going to fail in my efforts to get him the help he needed. He wanted help.

I realised that by asking for hospitalisation he might also have been trying to avoid going back to Trinity House. I believe that this was a factor in what he wanted. But I also believe that he was capable of killing himself in order to avoid Trinity House. He was really considering only hospital or killing himself. Trinity House was not an option for him.

To my knowledge, he had never yet attempted suicide, but my brother told me that the children of suicidal parents were at high risk. Joe Carney agreed and saw his suicide threats as serious.

On the way, I asked Brendan if he wanted to visit his grandmother in Eyrecourt, County Galway, as it would not be far out of our way. From the night when he had arrived at our house, he had talked a lot about her and how much he enjoyed going to see her.

The prospect of visiting her seemed to cheer him up a little. As well as giving him the chance to visit his grandmother, I also wanted to get more information about things he had been telling me, and to see how much I should rely on his word.

When we arrived at his grandmother's house in Eyrecourt, I could see the tenderness and love the woman showed toward her grandson. She was so happy that someone was trying to help him that she made me feel like a saint. She confirmed much of what Brendan had told me. After a very nice visit, we left her house for Ballinasloe.

We approached Ballinasloe with high hopes of getting help. The weather was very cold that day and showers of snow had started to fall. I felt nervous visiting a mental hospital as I had never been in one before.

I told the receptionist who I was and that I wanted to get Brendan admitted right away.

We were put in a large room with about twelve men in it. Brendan sat in a corner. I stayed standing, watching these twelve men who were all staring at us. A big man stood up and slowly made his way across the room towards me. He was over six feet tall and was looking at me very seriously. He put his hand on my arm, very gently, and asked me, 'Can I go home with you?'

I looked at him and thought to myself, 'Good Jesus, I'm doing everything possible to get one in — not take one out.' I looked over at Brendan in the corner. He was very pale from the cold, and shivering, but he had the beginnings of a smile on his face at my predicament.

At this point, a door opened and a doctor introduced himself to me. I told him what I wanted and he said he would talk to Brendan alone. He took him into another room and, in minutes, returned.

I was standing in the corridor now. He told me that he would have to admit Brendan. I told the doctor that Brendan had absconded from Trinity House detention centre in Dublin. He said that he didn't care where he had absconded from — that he had to admit him. He asked who would sign the admittance forms.

I said that I would. I was so pleased, I had tears in my eyes. Brendan had previously told me that they wouldn't take him in Ballinasloe as no one wanted him or wanted to give him help.

After some minutes, another doctor came in, and the first doctor went to talk to him. I was called into his office and told that they couldn't take him in but that there was a hospital in Galway city that would.

Now, I was almost crying with anger and I begged them to give him the help he so badly needed. He said that the place we were being sent to was a better place than Ballinasloe and was like a hotel.

I saw Joe Carney in the background and I could see the disappointment in his eyes. We didn't speak. Nor did we need to speak.

We came out of St Bridget's Hospital like two hungry, neglected dogs. I was shouting, 'Fuck every doctor in Ireland. Couldn't the stupid bastards see he badly needed help and it wouldn't cost a penny out of their pockets if they gave it to him? What is the State paying for?' I would hardly have gone to a mental hospital if I hadn't needed help.

Now, I don't think I would go at all.

Brendan was really down at this stage. He had no blood in his face. He just was so nervous, I cannot put it into words. Again he said, 'I told you they wouldn't help me.'

We started for Galway, and, to make it more depressing, the snow started again. It was nearly impossible to drive. Brendan was getting more depressed and said it was a waste of time driving to Galway. 'Nobody wants to help me,' he said.

I was wondering how we would face another mental hospital and how he would handle the same kind of treatment.

I was very much afraid that Brendan would jump out of the car and run away. I was aware of his young age and his physical fitness. He didn't seem to have anything to lose by running away. He was less than a month shy of his fifteenth birthday and a very fast cross-country runner. At one point, I had to stop the car and have a chat with him to calm him down. He didn't want to go to Galway.

After asking directions from several people, we finally arrived at St Anne's Hospital in Galway. During all this time, from about eight in the morning to about three in the afternoon, we hadn't eaten anything. I was afraid to stop, fearing that Brendan might run away.

When we arrived at the hospital in Galway, we were each given a cup of tea and a biscuit, and left waiting.

I spoke with two doctors and told them all I knew about Brendan. One of the doctors called Brendan's father. He agreed to come to the hospital.

The doctors told me that they would not make any decision until Michael Pat arrived. Later, there was another conversation with Michael Pat who said he couldn't come to the hospital but that he was giving his permission for the doctors to interview his son.

I spoke again to one of the doctors and I asked her to ask Brendan about his sexual abuse at Trinity House. She told me he was too disturbed to be questioned. They asked me to talk to Michael Pat on the phone, which I did. Michael Pat and I had had a row at one time, and we didn't like each other much.

The first thing he asked me was what the problem was. I said the problem was that he was supposed to come to Galway to sign the admittance papers and he hadn't come.

When I was with the doctors and Brendan, and while the doctors were questioning him, I asked a few questions in their presence about abuse. He wasn't inclined to answer except to say that he had been thumped. One of the doctors looked at me and I dropped the subject and let them talk without interruption.

Brendan had not yet told me the details of his sexual abuse but, from some things he said, I was fairly sure he had run away because of it. I was also convinced it played a part in his not wanting to go back.

The doctor finally said that she had spoken with the Trinity House people and that they had told her he wouldn't lose any points for having run away.

Just as it was getting dark, we started for home. I was hungry, fed up, and feeling like a complete failure. And, I was hoping that the cows were foddered so I wouldn't have to feed them in the dark.

I was so angry, I missed the road home between Galway city and Loughrea, and ended up in Clarenbridge. I had to retrace my steps to get on the right road.

Brendan saw how upset I was and offered to 'go back and do every day of my sentence and fuck the bastards.'

When we got to Woodford, I decided to drive the rest of the journey home by the mountain road through Derrygoolin. Little did I know then that it would be on this mountain road that Brendan would be arrested a little over five years later after one of the biggest man-hunts ever conducted in Ireland.

Indeed, we passed the very spot where he spent his last minutes outside prison. Between that day and his last minutes of freedom, he would never get the mental health care we had so desperately tried to obtain for him on that February day in 1989.

And I tried many more times.

When we got within ten miles of home, I called my wife on the CB my son had set up in the car. I told her most of what had happened. She tried to calm me down and told me that Garda O'Hara was waiting for me at the house.

Garda O'Hara had already spoken to the doctor at St Anne's Hospital in Galway and had already been contacted by Trinity House. The bad news was that Brendan would have to go back to the Dublin detention centre.

Later, I phoned JJ in New Orleans. He didn't hold out any hope for Brendan if he went back to Trinity House without proper mental health care.

It was decided that Brendan would have to return to Trinity House on Friday morning, 24 February. Instructions were left for me to call the detention centre on Thursday morning to make the arrangements about transportation. I talked to an administrator at Trinity House, and to the probation officer who said that she would come to the house and talk to Brendan.

I offered to drive Brendan back — a round trip of about 230 miles. A priest, Fr Tom McNamara visited to offer his help. When he left, Brendan said to me, 'What's he doing here? He's bent.' I asked him how he knew.

He grinned and said he knew and that he had served Mass for him. It was going from bad to worse by the minute.

I never saw a child cry like Brendan cried that night. He sobbed in my arms and he even made me cry. I never thought a child could have gone through so much in such a short life. I was very scared that as the time got closer for Brendan to return to Trinity House, he might do something drastic. I was afraid he would attempt suicide.

* * *

I had been so busy with Brendan that I was neglecting the farm animals, especially the cows that were ready to calve. On my return from Galway, my wife had told me that one of them was missing and must have gone into the forest to calve.

I couldn't search the forest that night because of the weather and darkness, so I waited until the next morning.

Next day, I found her dead. She was not able to finish calving, and the calf was dead too. She was a big loss, financially as well as emotionally. I wasn't in any state for more problems and was far from happy at knowing how both she and her calf must have suffered before they died.

Not only could I not see a light at the end of the tunnel — I couldn't even see the tunnel.

2

On the Run

Tony Muggivan

It was Friday and we were getting ready to bring Brendan back to Dublin. He was saying goodbye to everyone as I waited in the car. I noticed that there were no tears and he didn't seem a bit lonely — not like the night before.

We had to make a stop at the priest's house to pick up a package he wanted dropped off in Dublin. When I went into the house to get the package and the directions on where to drop it off, I left Brendan in the car outside.

When I came back to the car, there was no Brendan to be seen anywhere. Eventually I saw him in the distance.

I jumped into the car to try to cut him off. I shouldn't have tried to run after him though. He was a bronze medal winner for cross-country running.

Trying to catch Brendan in this area of Ireland was not easy. As I said, we live not far from the west shore of Lough Derg on the River Shannon. There are only a few miles of what is called 'good land' between the Shannon and the beginning of the Slieve Aughty mountains.

The Slieve Aughty mountains are not really mountains. They are more like a range of heathered hills and marshy valleys.

Because the area covered by these hills and valleys isn't much good for anything else, the State planted thousands of acres of it with trees — mostly pine trees —decades ago. Someone like Brendan could hide for a long time in these forests without getting caught. His only problem would be food, clothing, and shelter from the weather.

In all, there are about eighteen thousand acres of forest and a few hundred acres of privately owned woods in this area. All of these forests and woods overlook Lough Derg, and a journey from part of these wooded areas to a boat on the lake is very short. It could easily be travelled, night or day, without being seen.

If Brendan wanted to hide indefinitely, he would have little difficulty. And if he wanted to travel by boat the seven miles across to County Tipperary, he could also do that.

I returned home about mid-day and was telling my wife how very much Brendan was now outside the law. I told her I didn't think there was any way we could help him now. I felt disappointed but felt some relief that I had done as much as I could for him.

I called Trinity House and told them what had happened. I again talked to an administrator and told him about Brendan's fear of the detention centre. The administrator, like myself, was convinced that Brendan needed to be in a mental hospital and not at Trinity House.

I did some farm work, trying to get Brendan and his problems out of my mind, but wondering where he would go and what he would do. Now, the guards would have to catch him.

The weather was still very cold and wet. I finished all the outside work before it got dark, then came inside for my supper and settled down in the living room by the fire, to watch TV.

There are two doors to my house — a front door which we hardly ever use, and a door at the end of the house which comes directly into the kitchen at the end of the living room.

I went out of the living room to the kitchen for a cup of tea and sat at the table to drink it. I was still thinking about Brendan and wondering if I'd seen the last of him when I heard someone walking up to the back door. I looked up and saw the door opening, and in walked Brendan, soaked to the skin from the rain, acting as if there was nothing seriously wrong. Now we had a very serious problem but he didn't seem to be aware of it.

He told us he couldn't go back to Trinity House no matter what. I knew it would be a waste of time trying to convince him otherwise.

Next day, 25 February, Mary and I finally persuaded Brendan to tell us what had happened at Trinity House detention centre. He agreed on condition that Mary leave the room.

After she left, Brendan told me how a member of staff at the detention centre would lock him into his cell and sexually abuse him. He told me that this had started after he was there only a month, and that it had continued until about five or six weeks before he ran away. He told me in detail about the last incident.

The member of staff made him take his clothes off. He then pressed himself against Brendan's backside, reaching around with his hands to catch his penis. He then began to masturbate him.

In the course of the masturbation, which Brendan said was very painful, the skin was pulled back over the tip of his penis and it remained in that position because his penis swelled and the swelling wouldn't go down.

Brendan thought that his penis had been seriously injured. He went to the nurse for help, and she referred him to a doctor who gave him some cream, with directions on how to use it. Brendan said that he thought there was blood on his penis and that he still had marks and scars on it from what had happened.

I told him that he might have to be examined by doctors and a psychiatrist, and he agreed to this on condition that I would stay in the room while the examination was going on.

I contacted my solicitor, Billy Loughnane, through his partner, Margaret Hayes, and gave all the information to him. He asked for Brendan to be examined as soon as possible as the marks might soon go away. Later, I got a call from the garda sergeant in Scariff, asking me to talk to Brendan's father and see if we could work together.

On 27 February 1989, the Monday after Brendan had come back, and after I had reported the complaints of sexual abuse to Billy Loughnane, a guard stopped me on the road and asked me about Brendan. At this stage, I was in no humour to be nice to guards, or, for that matter, anyone in authority.

The guard asked me about missing chain saws, and reports of a house being broken into. He asked me whether I would know if Brendan might have anything to do with these reports. I told him I wouldn't know and suggested that the guards would be better occupied conducting investigations and asking questions about the reports of abuse Brendan had made. I told him that the real criminals might be getting paid by the State. When the guard got tired of listening to me, he went on his way.

At this stage, I had become alarmed at the prospect of helping anyone who would make Brendan go back to an institution where he could be harmed further.

On the night of 27 February, I decided to follow the suggestion I had received from the Scariff sergeant, that I visit Brendan's father. A letter for Michael Pat O'Donnell had arrived by mistake at my house and I decided to deliver it myself.

I met Michael Pat and his wife, Nora. They were both very angry at me and asked me where Brendan was. I told them I didn't know his whereabouts. Michael Pat said he would hold me responsible for his son and he wanted him back in Dublin right away.

A couple of days later, on 1 March 1989, the administrator I had previously spoken to called me from Trinity House, and told me he had heard the reports that Brendan was saying he had been sexually abused. I told him that Brendan had agreed to be examined by doctors and a psychiatrist.

I told him I did not know where Brendan was but believed him to be safe. I gave him the names of the staff member, and of the prisoner who had helped him, and asked that something be done about these two men.

He agreed to investigate both men and told me that Brendan had complained to him some time previously about being 'thumped' by the staff member whose name I had given him.

We knew that the guards could come at any time as they were likely to expect Brendan to return to where he had previously been welcome. We let him stay the night, but someone had to stay awake all night to watch out for the guards.

The following morning, I sent Brendan to a friend of mine, Sonny Farrell, and told him to stay there until he heard from me. Sonny Farrell was an old man who has since died. I didn't have the heart to force Brendan back to Trinity House, and I needed time to come up with a way to help him. Brendan persuaded Sonny Farrell to remove the window in his bedroom so that he could escape if the guards came.

In the next nine days, the garda squad car from Killaloe came to our house seven times inquiring about him. It started with guards and then went right up to the superintendent. All grades in the force were questioning me whenever they caught sight of me.

I began to have some idea of what it must have been like for my father when he was being watched and questioned by the British when he was in the old IRA from 1916 to 1921.

One of the times I was being questioned by the guards on the side of the road leading to my house, I glanced behind one of them and saw Brendan up near the top of a tree in the forest. I had warned him not to come near the place.

On another occasion, the guards were at my house, questioning me. Since they didn't seem to believe me when I said I didn't know where he was, I offered to let them search the house without a warrant. They declined and I found out later that had they come into the house, they could have found him hiding within three feet of where they were standing when they were questioning me.

I remained baffled about what to do since neither my wife nor I liked the idea of sending Brendan back to the detention centre. He had begun to play cat-and-mouse with the guards. Sometimes he would stay in a community hall across the street from the garda barracks in Mountshannon and would follow all the comings and goings of people at the barracks.

It was now into March, with the days getting longer but with the weather still staying cold and wet. I had a round-table discussion with all of my family, sons included, to discuss what to do.

Two of my sons had gone to school with Brendan in Mountshannon before he had got into difficulty with the law. Moreover, he was a second cousin of my children's, and everyone wanted to help him. We all wondered how we could.

Next morning, solicitor Billy Loughnane came to my house with my wife's brother-in-law, Tony O'Brien. He explained the law on how we might be able to help Brendan. He said that it would cost a lot of money. I called my brother and talked to Joe Carney. They both continued to advise me that mental health care was necessary no matter where Brendan went.

One day, I met Brendan on the road and he had a stick about four feet long. It was a stick cut from a young sally tree and it was pointed at both ends like a spear. It was over an inch in diameter. It looked like a very dangerous weapon.

I was angry when I saw it and told him to put it down, warning him never to let me see him with something like that again. Sonny Farrell told me he had seen him making it and was not happy at what he was doing.

I started to read a book I had taken from my brother's house when I had visited him in New Orleans in 1982. It was called *Abnormal Behavior*. While reading this book, I was thinking about Brendan. My concern was that if he were to continue on his present path, he could commit very serious crimes.

Meanwhile, my solicitor made arrangements with a barrister to take Brendan's case to court. We had decided to request the court that his sentence be set aside and that my wife and I be awarded custody.

Now there was a plan in place to get rid of the basis for one of Brendan's worst fears — the fear of going back to Trinity House.

He continued to live at Sonny Farrell's while waiting for the court hearing in County Carlow. It was scheduled for 17 April 1989.

Going to court was expensive but we felt we had to help Brendan. I had mixed feelings about the courts and the State. On the one hand, I was grateful to the courts, but, on the other hand, I was fed up with the State.

Although I was proposing to save the State a lot of money by taking Brendan off its hands, I had to pay for the legal expenses myself — a total of two thousand pounds. When I visited Billy Loughnane the day before court, I gave him fourteen hundred pounds and hoped that it was worth it.

Fr Tom McNamara visited my house on the same day. I needed a letter of consent from Brendan's father but I couldn't get it myself as Michael Pat and I were on bad terms. Fr McNamara got it for me and brought it to me, signed, so we were all ready for court.

I continued to have serious worries about Fr McNamara's involvement. One night, before going to court, we were sitting in the living room — Mary, myself, Brendan, and the priest. Mary went into a downstairs bedroom, one room away from where we were sitting. At the time, she was suffering from a badly injured back and frequently had to rest because of pain.

The phone rang in the front room and I went to answer it, leaving Brendan and the priest alone in the living room. I was talking on the phone while half-listening to the conversation going on between the priest and Brendan. I suddenly froze when I heard Fr McNamara say, 'I love you, Brendan.'

I didn't know what to do. When I walked into the sitting room, Brendan looked at me. It was so sad to see a man, up in years, in love with a young boy, and to see the distress it was causing the latter. I sent Brendan out of the kitchen and continued talking to the priest as if I hadn't heard what I'd heard.

When the priest left, I asked my wife if she had heard it too. She had. The priest always wanted Brendan sitting near him and several times I had seen him putting his hand on Brendan's inner thigh. I warned Brendan and told him to make sure to avoid ever being alone with him. I warned the priest too about danger if he didn't behave himself. In those days, it was a waste of time going to the higher-ups in the Church or to the guards.

The priest had known Brendan since his childhood. Brendan had regularly served Mass for him when he was younger. For many years, parents had warned their children never to be alone with this priest.

Fr McNamara later told me of an occasion when Brendan had visited him at the rectory, having been out in the rain. He said he had to have Brendan strip naked so that he could dry his clothes before the fire.

I talked to Brendan about my worries and he told me he had known for a long time that the priest was 'bent'. I later found out from Fr McNamara that, over a period of time, he had given Brendan substantial amounts of money. When I heard this, I wondered if Brendan had been blackmailing him.

I did not like what I heard but I knew it was useless to report the priest since, over a period of many years, many reports had been made and nothing had been done. In spite of this, I did complain to the guards, and anyone else who would listen to me.

24

One day, I had an argument with a guard about why Fr McNamara was never investigated and how worried I was for Brendan. The guard told me that if I saw what he had on the 'station book' about the priest in question, I would be shocked.

I talked to Fr McNamara later and warned him that if he didn't distance himself from Brendan that Brendan would be capable of cutting his throat and laughing at him while he was doing it. I think I scared him for awhile.

Brendan was in danger of abuse in Trinity House — and in Mountshannon, from an unlikely source.

However, I needed Fr McNamara for a few more days — until court was over. So I had to walk a thin line. I couldn't afford to stay completely away from him.

Even though we were trying our best to do whatever we could to prevent Brendan from ever having to go back to the detention centre, we had begun wondering whether he was already harmed beyond the point of being able to recover.

3

Fostering Brendan

Tony Muggivan

At this time, one of my wife's brothers, Dermot O'Sullivan, was told by his employer that he had a job for Brendan in Shannon. The name of the factory was Fabricated Products. Dermot had worked there for years.

I asked Dermot to come to Carlow Court with us and testify that Brendan had a chance of good employment and training. I had already told our barrister about the promised job. Our solicitor, Billy Loughnane, had already been given the letters we had collected.

There was a letter from Joe Carney, stating his belief that Brendan would be better off in my custody. There was also a letter from one of Brendan's former teachers, James Collins, who described Brendan's school experiences and gave a history of some of his early distress. He also said that Brendan would be better off in my custody and the custody of my family.

There was a letter from Fr McNamara and the consent letter signed by Brendan's father, which the priest had obtained. The following is what Jim Collins, Brendan's last teacher, had to say about him:

Brendan O'Donnell was a pupil [at Mountshannon] from 1–4–85 to 30–06–87. For approximately two years, that is April 85 to March 87, his behaviour gave no cause for concern in the school. He presented no discipline problems to me or any of the staff. He took part in all school activities with interest — most especially in hurling where he showed some talent.

In fact, in June 1987 he helped the school win our section in the primary schools hurling championship by scoring two goals in the final. At school he also played football and took part in cross-country running. To the best of my recollection, he holds a bronze medal for the team competition in the Clare Schools Championship.

The one area where he differed from most pupils was that he seemed rather suspicious of everybody at school and I would say he found it difficult to place his trust in other people.

From about April 1987, until he left us the following June, he certainly gave us much cause for concern. He appeared to be suffering from anxiety or depression. He was often crying for no apparent reason. He suffered from pains in his stomach, which, since medical people could not find anything wrong with him, would seem to have been psychological in nature. In any event he began not turning up in school and disappeared from home for periods.

His attendance at school improved somewhat when, by arrangement with his father, he returned to school on a regular basis until his confirmation was over. After that, while regular attendance ceased, he came when hurling was involved . . .

. . . Initially, he told me that the reason he couldn't stop crying was that his father was not bringing the family on a visit to England around Easter 1987 to see his younger brother. Brendan always gave the impression of being attached to him. I suspect, however, that this alone was not the cause of his upset.

It is my opinion that Brendan felt a very deep sense of loss when his mother died, and the void left by her death has never been filled. I feel Brendan needs professional help but I feel equally importantly that he needs the comfort of a loving and caring family environment to help him recover something from a shattered childhood. What he certainly does not need is incarceration in an institution.

Jim Collins's letter contains the main reasons given to the court in support of foster care with me rather than returning to Trinity House.

I travelled to Carlow, which is almost on the other side of Ireland from where we live. My wife and Fr McNamara were with me. Brendan travelled with his cousin, Josephine O'Brien, and her husband, Tony O'Brien. He was too frightened to travel in my car as he was afraid it would be recognised by the guards.

We had not been bothered by the guards since it had become known that there was a court date, but Brendan continued to be afraid of them. Moreover, I did not want him in the same car with the priest. The Killaloe superintendent, Con McCarthy, also came to court.

The court session lasted about one hour. Our barrister talked to the judge and told him about the letters. Then, I gave my account of what I knew, and Dermot told the court about the job in Shannon.

The judge granted the request for foster care, put Brendan on probation instead of sending him back to Trinity House, and ordered him to appear in court in Nenagh, County Tipperary, at the Michaelmas session in September 1989.

When we came out to the yard after court, I had a talk with Superintendent McCarthy. I told him what I had heard about the abuse at Trinity House and Clonmel. He promised to send an officer to my house to start an investigation.

I was pleased with the outcome of the court but I was disappointed that the judge didn't give an order for counselling or any kind of mental health care. I was hoping that Joe Carney would be appointed to counsel Brendan and that, if necessary, he would be hospitalised for a while.

We all went to a hotel in Carlow for a meal before heading back home. I was concerned when I saw Fr McNamara arrange to sit next to Brendan. After we had almost finished eating, I couldn't believe my eyes when I saw the priest again put his hand on Brendan's inner thigh.

I got Brendan's attention and signalled to him to move away from the priest. Before he could move, however, Fr McNamara asked him to go for a walk with him around the town of Carlow. I stayed close behind them, watching to make sure that nothing more would happen. It was a nightmare to be keeping an eye on the priest all of the time, while, at the same time, trying to help Brendan deal with his fear of the guards. I had previously informed the guards in Killaloe about the complaints against Trinity House and the beatings in Clonmel. Superintendent McCarthy acted immediately though, and, very soon after I talked to him, a detective was sent to investigate.

After several hours of questioning Brendan, the detective talked to Mary and me and told us he had no doubt about the truth of Brendan's story. However, he phoned me four to six weeks later and told me that the case could not be proven and would have to be dropped. I was later told by an administrator at Trinity House that the staff member had resigned.

Brendan remained very nervous, and was especially so whenever he saw a garda car. I now had to worry about coming up with the rest of the money for the solicitor, which I managed to do in the following few days.

I hadn't been making much money on the farm, or doing extra work for additional money, because of all the time I had been spending on Brendan and the court case. I had to begin hoping that the cows that hadn't calved yet would all have twins and that help would come from somewhere. But the cows didn't have twins and I had to work for the help.

I was, however, hoping that everything would now settle down. In the days after court, we relaxed more, and Brendan went shopping with my wife. She bought him a knitted pullover with a rope design which he really liked. One day, he came home and told me he had met a guard who didn't stop him and question him. I told him that he had nothing to fear from the guards any more.

After some time, he seemed happy. But sometimes, when I thought I had reassured him, he would ask me again if I thought they would come after him again. It drove me crazy trying to explain to him that he was safe. The other thing that drove everybody in the house crazy was his cleanliness. He never drank a cup of tea without checking the cup to see if it was clean. He would wash the cups before drinking from them. One day, my son, Brendan, got angry with him and rubbed a slice of bread on the kitchen floor and then ate it. He told Brendan to watch how it wouldn't kill him.

Brendan bonded very well with my wife. He would sit in the kitchen and talk to Mary for long hours while she was doing the household chores. He would frequently make tea for her and, when she was bed-ridden with her back, he would bring tea to her before she got up in the morning.

He learned how to drive the tractor, and this caused some jealousy between him and my two older children, Brendan and Kevin. My two younger sons were too young to drive, or learn to drive, so they were not as bothered by him. When there was work to be done, Brendan O'Donnell would try to avoid it.

In the morning time, the cows would have to be brought into the shed to be milked at about 7.30 or 8.00. One of my sons would be expected to get up early and bring in the cows. Brendan never wanted to get up, and by the time he did get up, someone else would have brought them in. He was unwilling to do any work. This was resented by my sons, even by the younger ones.

There was a German who came to the village every year for about twenty years. His name was Hans Mollidor, and he was a good friend of mine. When he came to the village, I would spend a lot of time fishing with him on the lake. He died a few years ago.

Hans was a very kind man and liked hiring the children to do work around his house. He would pay them ten pounds a day for their work, even though the children would spend more time playing, fishing and eating, than they did working.

The work consisted mostly of collecting dead branches from around his house and burning them. This meant making big fires which the children loved. For the children, his visits were like a holiday. At the end of the day, Hans would line up the boys and give them their pay. He would have the money in his wallet and, when he gave them their pay, they could see that he carried a lot of cash. He had a very nice Mercedes and would often take the boys for drives.

Brendan started to work for him but would never eat any food at his house. He always came home early for his meals. Even though he worked shorter days, he still got all of his pay. The food at Hans's house consisted mostly of noodles and cheese. I had it many times and found it delicious. Hans would prepare the food and enjoy watching the children eat.

One evening, Brendan came to me and said that he wanted to buy a scrambler motor bike — an old one that would cost about five hundred pounds. I told him he had no money for the bike. He said that he would get a job and earn the money. I promised that if he saved a good deal of the money for the bike I would help him with the rest.

My oldest son had a scrambler bike, but it was completely broken and finished. My sons had had good fun with it on the farm though. I got Brendan a job at two pounds an hour working for Norbert Hau who lived in Cloonamerrin. Cloonamerrin is a townland not far from Mountshannon and about two miles from my home.

Brendan left the house at nine o'clock every morning and came home at about 2.20 p.m. A few times when I visited, I watched him working from Norbert Hau's kitchen. He worked as if he had a bag of cement on his back. You really wouldn't see what he had done by the time evening came.

As the days went by, he was getting up later and later. As the money got less and less, the idea of the bike came to an end. I noticed that he was also coming home earlier and earlier in the afternoons. At the time, I believed he was just lazy and didn't want to work.

Years later, Norbert told me that he was never able to get Brendan to eat anything from the time he arrived until the time he left. This meant that Brendan would eat breakfast, walk two miles to Norbert Hau's, work a few hours, and then walk back the two miles to my home without having eaten since breakfast.

The two miles back to my home are mostly uphill, especially the last mile. When I heard from Norbert that Brendan had not been eating, I realised how much stress he must have been under from his fear of germs in food, and how much he had to endure because of this fear.

Norbert later told me that Brendan had been caught entering a nearby house and stealing apples and bananas. It seems that he did not have the same fear of germs in fruit. I now realise that he was trying to hide his unusual fear from everyone.

There were so many incidents with Brendan throughout the summer of 1989, it would be impossible to tell them all. He wanted a lot of attention from me. He talked a lot about guns — Russian guns, American guns — almost always about army guns. I would try to change the subject but was never very successful.

One day, I took down one of my guns — a three-shot semi-automatic — and said to Brendan, 'Come on, let's see what a good shot you are.' He told me to take it away, saying that he had got into enough trouble over guns. I knew that he did not really want me to take it away.

I had some idea of why he had been institutionalised but I did not know all the details. Later, my brother, JJ, interviewed a number of people, including Brendan, about what had happened.

According to Ann Marie O'Donnell, at the end of 1987, when her brother was thirteen, he was passing a workman who was laying a cement footpath. The cement had been laid already, but was still wet, and the workman was standing near to a pile of sand. When Brendan walked by, he kicked sand onto the wet concrete with his foot. An argument followed, in the course of which Brendan kicked more sand onto the concrete. As Brendan was kicking the sand, the workman put a shovel in front of his leg, causing Brendan to hit the shovel with his shin.

Brendan's injury may have been caused by a combination of the man swinging the shovel and Brendan kicking. Ann Marie maintained that Brendan had kicked the sand to annoy the workman, whereas Brendan's account, as related to JJ, was that the workman had deliberately hit him with the shovel and that he was innocent of any wrongdoing.

In any event, Brendan was enraged and threw rocks into the workman's yard. He later left his house and went to the home of a man named Denis Tuohy from whom he stole a gun and some cartridges. On his way back to his home with the gun, he met an elderly man, Michael Ames, whom he confronted, threatening to shoot him if he did not get down on his knees.

Brendan then proceeded home, firing a shot in the air and a shot in the direction of the workman's house. The guards were called and Brendan was eventually arrested and sent to St Michael's in Finglas, Dublin. He was later transferred to Clonmel in County Tipperary.

The incident represented the end of Brendan's school career and the beginning of his institutional care. As JJ concluded, it was a major turning point in Brendan's life. It set him on a dangerous, destructive course, and he seemed unable to change direction.

Brendan told JJ that during one of his assessments after his arrest, he found himself alone in the room, and walked behind the examiner's desk to see what was being written about him. According to Brendan, the examiner had written that he was depressed.

JJ asked Brendan about his stay at the reform school in Clonmel. Brendan told him that he was beaten badly at this school, and he gave a detailed description of the strap which he said was used. He said that he was punched in the face many times. He ran away on a number of occasions and was eventually sent to Trinity House in Dublin.

At the time, I knew none of these details, but I put the gun away and was always careful that both the gun and ammunition were properly secured in different places. My son, Brendan, told me later that he remembered how Brendan would spend much of his time in school drawing pictures of guns. This was not long before he confronted the people in Whitegate and fired the shots.

My sister-in-law, Vera O'Sullivan, started a small business buying and selling young goslings. This business required that someone be available to answer phone calls from buyers. Brendan took over the task and performed it very well. He would sit on the couch with the phone and carefully write down all of the phone messages and orders. He was very exact about the job and I still have notes he took while performing it.

He talked a lot about keeping physically fit. He would say, 'You have to keep fit in case you have to go on the run.' He never seemed to get over the idea that he should always be ready to go on the run, escape from someone, particularly the guards, or be ready to defend himself. He seemed to live with fear, whether fear of germs getting into his food or on his hands, or fear of the guards.

One day, when he was talking about being fit and ready to go on the run, I said to him, 'Come on — let me see what a good runner you are.' I was about forty-eight years old at the time. We lined up in a field, agreeing to run a race of about fifty yards. He got a shock when I was able to stay neck and neck with him.

When we finished in a tie, he looked at me and said, 'Jaysus, you're a tough fucker.' He had a sense of humour about being beaten and didn't talk too much after that about what a good runner he was!

I was away one day and before I left, I gave him, Kevin and my son Brendan, some work to do on the farm. Brendan O'Donnell wanted to drive the tractor all day and not do any of the rough work. My son Brendan finally got fed up and confronted him. They both got into a hard fist fight. It ended in a standoff with both of them agreeing to shake hands. I heard about the fight later and thought it a positive sign that they had made up like grown-ups.

Brendan was very wary of any kind of physical contact. You could never leave your hand on his shoulder. He would be inclined to cringe away from you. For example, I did a little judo when I was a young man in England. I tried to teach Brendan a few of the judo moves, but it was impossible to get close to him to teach him.

I sometimes lent the children the boat to go fishing on the lake. I would never send my youngest son, Ross, alone with him as he was small for his age. I always sent Gerard with Ross, as Gerard was big and strong for his age and would protect Ross. On JJ's advice, I was not for taking too many chances.

Brendan sometimes would ask me to lend him Hans Mollidor's cruiser. This boat had cost fourteen thousand pounds — second hand — and I was responsible for taking care of it. There was no way anybody was getting it. I took them out in it several times and let them all drive it. I believe I gave them all a good time. I used to tell them jokingly that my home was more like a holiday home.

My sons used to play hurling but Brendan never showed any interest. Before he was institutionalised he had been a remarkably good hurler and athlete. Now, he seemed unable to compete or even to join with my sons in any activity. Every chance he got, he would be in the kitchen talking to Mary.

By this time, Mary was having a lot of problems with her back, and she had to go into hospital for an operation. Before she went, Brendan took good care of her and was really worried about her. He used to make tea and toast for her. He told me a lot about his own mother and the way that she had died. He said that she had taken her own life.

Apparently Brendan's mother had died in hospital when she was having her womb removed. He said that he never believed that though. According to Brendan, she must have got hold of tablets from the nurses' tray, saved them up, and taken them all at one time.

Regarding the mother's suicide attempts, JJ would later interview both Brendan and his sister, Ann Marie. According to the latter, there were numerous suicide attempts.

At the age of sixteen, Brendan gave JJ a surprisingly detailed account of a suicide attempt that had occurred when he was between three and four years of age. He said that he had seen his mother trying to get out of bed in a dazed state. She had fallen to the floor, hitting her face on a locker beside the bed, and her nose was bleeding as she hit the floor. Brendan said that his mother was unable to get up from the floor, which was now covered with blood. He went for help.

The mother was taken shortly afterwards to a hospital in Ennis, County Clare, where she remained for several months. The children reported hearing later that their mother had attempted to kill herself by taking all of her medicine and drinking a half bottle of whiskey.

This is probably the suicide attempt referred to by Doctor Ledwith when he testified at Brendan's trial.

Margaret O'Donnell died in a hospital on 28 January 1984 when Brendan was almost ten years old, Anne Marie was about thirteen and a half, and the youngest child was seventeen months old. Brendan's older brother was eleven at the time. The cause of death was reportedly a blood clot that broke loose from Margaret's leg and went to her lungs when she was recovering from surgery.

Initially Brendan believed that his mother was not dead and that it was somebody else's body in the morgue. During the actual burial, he tried to jump into the grave to save her, saying that she was alive and would be smothered by the clay that was being shovelled onto her coffin.

At the end of May, my wife, Mary, went into hospital and I believe that Brendan was lost without her. I tried to take the children to visit her as often as I could. It was a round trip of about a hundred and ten miles from my home to the hospital, and I was driving to visit her with some of the children three or four times a week. This meant I was away from home a lot. Brendan had less time with either myself or Mary.

During all this time, I had only one visit from a probation officer. I got no help from any other source. To keep a child in detention costs about five hundred pounds per week, yet the State gives no help when you take a child into your home. Brendan received no counselling or any other kind of mental health care.

4

In Trouble Again

Tony Muggivan

I noticed that Brendan was beginning to go to bed earlier and earlier in the evening. Many times, there would be a good film on TV or the other children would have picked up a good video to watch. I would ask Brendan to stay up with the family and to watch either the film or the video. He would prefer to go to bed.

He told me that when he was at Trinity House all they ever did was watch movies all the time. I noticed that he seemed to have seen every movie that ever came on the TV.

I also noticed that Brendan was getting very quiet, but I knew there was nothing that I could do.

At the time, I did not realise that a friend of mine, Denis Woods, was also very worried about Brendan. Denis visited us on one occasion during the spring of 1989, when our children and Brendan were playing football in the yard. The ball was kicked in Denis's direction and he kicked it back towards Brendan O'Donnell. Brendan was not expecting the ball and it hit him on the chest. Denis later told JJ that he saw a look of rage in Brendan O'Donnell's eyes and felt, at that moment, that Brendan was capable of killing.

My middle son, Kevin, recalled an evening, shortly after dusk, when he and Brendan had been on their way to a neighbour's house on an errand. Brendan had suddenly, in a frightened voice, pointed toward a bush and asked Kevin if he could see the man standing under it. Brendan was so sure that there was a dangerous man standing under the bush that he caused Kevin to imagine he could see him too. Both boys began to move rapidly and quietly away from what they both now believed was a dangerous man following them. Eventually, they met the neighbour they had been on their way to visit and he escorted them home.

One Saturday, I was going to visit Mary in the hospital. Brendan came to me and asked if he could visit his mother's grave. He wanted to cycle the four miles to Clonrush where the grave was. I felt very unhappy with the idea and reluctantly said yes. But I warned him to be back early, as it would be dark when I got home.

When I got home, it was very late and there was no sign of Brendan. I waited up for him, but he didn't come home. Next morning, I heard that a car belonging to a man named Maxie Bogenberger, had been stolen and crashed near Whitegate.

I knew immediately who was responsible.

Brendan arrived home about 11.30 the following morning. I asked him where he had been. He said that he had stayed in a hay shed overnight. When I asked him why he had not come home, he said he didn't know. I asked him if he had stolen Maxie's car and crashed it. He said that he had not.

He had a pair of industrial leather gloves, which I took from him. I told him that I was going to give them to the guards, and that they would be able to find stains of old paint from the car and connect him to the theft. I went to another room and put the gloves away.

When I came back, I told him that it would go better for him in court if he admitted to the guards that he had taken the car. After a long time, he admitted to having stolen it. He said that he had been driving too fast, and had crashed on a bend.

When I asked why he had taken the car, he said that he wanted to bring his sister, Ann Marie, to England. He told me that she was very unhappy at home. I phoned Superintendent McCarthy at his home and told him the story. He had given me his number in case I ever needed his help. He was the only official I came to know ever to do this.

Superintendent McCarthy was very nice and calm and spoke at length to Brendan on the phone. He said he would call to my home on the following Monday and talk about it.

When he came, we had a long talk. He said the car was old and perhaps I could pay for it as Brendan might have learned his lesson. He was very reluctant to have him return to Trinity House as he felt they were giving him no psychological care. He came back a short time later and said that Maxie wanted three thousand pounds for the car.

It was completely out of the question for me to come up with that much money. I still owed Michael O'Sullivan, my brother-in-law, some money I had borrowed for the court case in April, and I was getting more concerned about Brendan.

I had a Persian cat, a very gentle animal. I think the cat thought he was a dog. He always came looking at the cattle with me, night or day. He used to sleep in an outside shed at the time and I could never look at a cow at night without his hearing me and coming with me.

The kitchen window had a small window at the top. The cat would jump up on the window and hold on to the top of the pane with his front paws and start to meow when he wanted to get in. If I said come, he would come. If I said no, he would stay. The back door is still, to this day, scratched from his nails. From the time he came to live with us, Brendan was amused by the cat, and talked quite a bit about him.

One day, the cat disappeared. I always believed that Brendan had done away with it. Kevin, my son, found a small axe in the forest about seventy yards from the house. The axe was mine. I asked Brendan about the cat and if he had seen it. He said that he had not, but he made no attempt to find it.

During all this time, I was in constant touch with my brother in New Orleans. He was very concerned at what I told him about the cat.

Later, it emerged that in the period after Margaret O'Donnell's death, there had been reports of Brendan's having been cruel towards younger children in school and towards animals. It was said that he had persuaded younger children in the school to walk into nettles to search for a lost ball. The children had got stung and had cried, and Brendan had laughed at them.

One local said that she had been aware of Brendan hanging two kittens on the clothesline in the yard. A local seven-year-old had been disturbed at the sight and had run to her mother screaming. Again, Brendan had laughed.

According to medical reports presented at the trial, Margaret O'Donnell had told Dr Ledwith in July 1979 that Brendan was very afraid of animals.

The day came when Brendan and I had to go to court in Nenagh. This was the Michaelmas Session of the Circuit Court, held at the very beginning of September 1989, in Nenagh. Nenagh is a town in County Tipperary, about twenty-five miles away by road from my house but much shorter across the lake. In fact, at night, we can see the lights of the town from near where I live.

I got up early to do the farm work before leaving for Nenagh. I called Brendan to get ready. It was a beautiful morning.

I had lent him a new Aran pullover of mine, so that he would look well. Just before we left, he said he wanted to go to the toilet. I waited a long time for him to come out. Finally, I called him, but there was no answer.

I called a couple of times and then started to worry that he had cut his throat with a blade. I broke in the door but he was gone with my new pullover.

I began cursing him to myself, wondering how I was going to explain in court why I couldn't produce him. I drove to Nenagh and met with my solicitor, with Superintendent McCarthy, and with another officer.

They were disappointed. I was sent to a garda station across from the court to phone home to see if he had returned. It was decided that if he had returned, a Garda Lowry would drive over to Mountshannon for him.

However, he had not returned. As anticipated, the judge ordered a bench warrant for his arrest.

Brendan was on the run again. He could not stop running. From what, I don't know.

I drove home, thinking about how all this had happened in such a short time. It was only about six months since I had first met him. Late that night, as I was sitting down, the back door opened and in walked Brendan.

He wanted to know how the court had gone. He was in no way surprised at the outcome, saying simply, 'So I'm on the run.' I would like to have been able to tell him I didn't care, but I couldn't. I told him that the guards had orders to arrest him and that he couldn't stay at my home any more.

Before coming home from court that day, I had talked with Superintendent McCarthy and we had both agreed to a plan for his arrest. According to the plan, I would let him sleep at my house and he would send two officers to arrest him at two or three in the morning when he would be asleep. The officers would pretend to be angry with me for keeping or hiding him.

It was a very emotional night for me and for my family. The two officers arrived very quietly and I showed them to the bedroom where Brendan and my son were asleep. They woke him up gently. He asked them what they wanted.

When they said they were here to arrest him, he asked them 'Can't you come back in the morning'. I couldn't believe it.

One officer was being a little angry at me — as planned. Brendan looked so relaxed and agreeable that they didn't bother to handcuff him. They were also sensitive to the fact that my children were present.

As we came down the stairs, he was between the two officers. One officer moved a little too far ahead, giving Brendan an opportunity to escape. In a second, he was gone like a shot back up the stairs and out a window.

Of course, he knew the layout of the house and the surrounding area, even in the dark. They had no chance of catching him.

I felt so sorry for them that I told them I would explain to Superintendent McCarthy what had happened, which I did.

This was the last time Brendan stayed at my house. He was now on a downward spiral. He was a fifteen-and-a-half-year-old teenager out of control.

Brendan lived rough for a day before he came back looking for food. We waited to let him settle down. Then he stole two hundred pounds from my son, Kevin. Kevin kept the money in a box in his bedroom.

On 3 September, he stole Denis Tirnan's car. Denis arrived at my home within twenty minutes of discovering that his car was gone. We took off after him. I was in contact with Killaloe garda station, and we drove to Portumma.

I was out driving all night and at about three in the morning, I again contacted Killaloe station. They reported no sighting of him. The guard on duty told me to get a couple of hours' sleep. The guards were also searching for him. I started driving the forest roads and went to high points to see if I could pick out the headlamps of a car.

At about 6.30 in the morning, I found the car burning. The front wheel had come off the road and, as it was a front-wheel drive, Brendan had been unable to get it back on the road. As it happens, this was the entrance to the forest road where the bodies of his victims were found over four years later.

I had to go and tell Denis and his sister Rose that their car was burned out. Naturally, they were upset. There was stuff in the car that their late father, a boat-builder, had made and, of course, it had been burned. They had to replace the car at their own expense.

A few days later, Brendan came back to my house and agreed to return to Trinity House if the people from there came for him and not the guards. I phoned the detention centre and it was agreed that a car would be sent down from Dublin to Mountshannon for him.

I called Joe Duffy, a supervisor in the forest. I told him I needed Denis Woods to help with Brendan until he was picked up by the people from Trinity House. The journey from Dublin to my house takes about three hours by car.

Denis came to the house and stayed with Brendan for several hours, talking to him. Brendan said that he knew that Denis was there to prevent him from running away again.

When the Trinity House officers came for him, Brendan seemed happy to see them. I believe that he was happy he wasn't going to jail. He returned with them to Dublin.

About six weeks after returning to Trinity House, in November 1989, Brendan was released on a weekend pass. He again failed to return after his pass had expired. Instead, he went on the rampage.

He stole Marcus Bogenberger's car. Marcus Bogenberger is the son of Maxie Bogenberger from whom he had stolen his first car after Mary had gone to hospital. Brendan was driving around for a few days in this car and hid it in Tim Reeves' cattle yard for a while. Tim Reeves notified Garda O'Hara but when the guard came to see the car some time later, it was gone.

While driving Marcus Bogenberger's car, Brendan passed my son, Brendan, on the road, but he didn't stop or talk to him. A short time later, he was driving on a narrow road near our home (Carroll's Road) when he was met by Sean Allen. I think Marcus Bogenberger was travelling in the car with Sean Allen. When Brendan saw who they were, he jumped out of the car he was driving and ran into the forest. Marcus got his undamaged car back.

Brendan remained in the area. The next car he stole and crashed was Kinneallys'. Interestingly, he stole this car from outside Fr Tom McNamara's house. Why he was there when he had previously tried to keep away from the priest, I do not know.

Brendan was finally arrested at Shannon Airport, trying to escape to England. Prior to that, he had broken into Hans Mollidor's house from where he had stolen whisky and a leather jacket. In breaking into Mollider's house, he smashed a big, double-glazed window. The window let off a loud, explosive bang. Locals came to the house when they heard the noise but there was no sign of anyone when they got there.

I got a call about it straightaway. I went to Mollidor's with my son, Brendan, and brother-in-law, Dermot O'Sullivan. We searched the woods. The guards arrived about thirty minutes later. Hans had a lot of tools in the house, and I remember one guard asking me if there was a Hilty nail gun in the house. I said that there wasn't. It's interesting, however, that a guard considered him dangerous even in 1989. At close range, a Hilty nail gun can be a dangerous weapon.

Brendan must have been hungry and cold that night. There was no food in the house, but he had taken a bottle of whisky and a coat anyway. Taking the whisky was unusual for him since he didn't like drink very much.

Denis Woods and I stayed all night in Mollidor's house. Although it was very cold, we couldn't switch on the central heating as it would have made too much noise. I thought he might come back and I was afraid that he would set fire to the house. We already knew that he would always try to destroy evidence that could connect him to a crime.

Some time later, I met Denis Woods and I noticed that he had a limp. I asked him what had happened and he told me that he had hit his knee off a wall next to his bed while he was asleep. Denis later told JJ that he had, in fact, had a disturbing dream in which both Brendan and I featured.

In this dream, Denis heard the phone ringing and went to answer it. It was me on the line, and I told him that Brendan was in the forest about seventy yards across from the front of my house, and that he had a gun and was planning to shoot someone. I asked him to go into the forest to talk to Brendan and persuade him to give up the gun. After much debate, Denis agreed to see what he could do and drove to my house, and, at my direction, walked into the forest. When he entered the forest, he saw Brendan standing near a tree with a gun in his hands. He tried to persuade him to give up the gun and to come out of the forest. Thinking that Brendan was going to do what he asked him to do, Denis turned to walk from the forest, expecting Brendan to follow him. Just as he turned to walk away, he heard the click of the safety catch being released on the gun and believed that he was about to be shot.

Denis felt himself jump with fear in his sleep. When he jumped, he hit his knee off the wall beside his bed, badly bruising it, and rendering himself barely able to walk for several days.

It was a strange feeling to be hiding out on Dooras Hill with a loaded double-barrel shotgun in my hands all night. I thought I was going crazy. Moreover, I had a loaded gun in my hands to protect myself against a fifteen-and-a-half-year-old boy. Denis Woods was with me and was also wondering what Brendan might do next. Brendan had put fear into us all. Because he was scared, we were scared of what he might do to escape whatever it was that frightened him.

He was on the run again and trying desperately to escape. He found his way to Shannon Airport. Shannon Airport is about thirty-five miles from Mountshannon. He was arrested trying to get a ticket to England.

48

After his arrest, he was charged with the theft and burning of Denis Tirnan's car and with breaking into Hans Mollidor's house. I was in court in Shannon when he was charged.

The judge ordered him sent back to Trinity House to await trial. Trial was scheduled for a later date and was to be held in Tulla, County Clare.

I was feeling down after saying goodbye to him in the Shannon court and an older guard came over to console me. He advised me that when Brendan returned to my house, I should take him out to the mountain shooting, and get him interested in things like that.

I wondered whether I would ever come back if I took him out to the mountain. The last thing I wanted in his hands was a gun. I had my guns hidden all the time he was with me. But God bless the old guard for his good intentions.

Dr Gerry O'Neill saw Brendan again, in August 1989, after his return to Trinity House, and found no evidence of psychosis, although he did appear vulnerable and displayed poor judgement and a diminished sense of conscience and of right and wrong.

In January 1990, Dr O'Neill again interviewed Brendan. This time he believed him to be very truthful and felt that he spoke 'from the heart'. On this occasion, Brendan was subdued and depressed about his mother's death. He admitted to Dr O'Neill that some of the stories he had previously told him were contrived, but said that he had half-believed they were true. The doctor found that Brendan had a fantastic view of the future and saw himself in prison in five years' time. He had no friends, no ambition to work and had low self-esteem. He seemed, in the words of the doctor, 'a sad, lonely boy'.

Brendan told Dr O'Neill that he thought himself to be mad, as he could not understand some of his own behaviour. The doctor believed that he had reached 'the real Brendan' and that Brendan was, probably for the first time, discussing his real feelings.

Two guards from here went to Trinity House to question Brendan about the break-in at Hans Mollider's house. Brendan later told me that one of these guards told him that I was no friend of his and that I had set him up to be arrested at my house the night he had run away from the two guards.

Telling him this, of course, broke any bond of trust he had with me. He was never very trusting to start with. Later, after he was released from prison, I got a phone call at eleven o'clock one night. The person on the phone warned me to leave Brendan O'Donnell alone. He said that if I didn't, he would 'get' someone close to me. 'I won't bother you,' he said. 'But I will get someone close to you.'

I knew Brendan's voice and I believed it was him on the phone. I was very concerned and kept the gun as close to me as possible until I met him and talked to him to see how bad he was. I confronted him about the phone call. He denied having made it.

After the court session in Shannon, I didn't see Brendan again until he came down to court in Tulla, County Clare, to answer the charges against him. I believe it was early in February 1990. Brendan was now only a month shy of his sixteenth birthday.

When I saw him in court, I had a chance to talk to him. I noticed bandages on his wrist. We had only a short time to talk and I didn't get a chance to ask him about it.

As far as I can remember, he had the next court session in Ennis for the additional charges. I was there but I got a chance to say only a few words to him. He was sentenced to some extra time.

He was back in Trinity House and I had to go to one more court session in the Circuit Court in Waterford. Justice Sheridan was the judge. At this stage, he must have been tired of looking at me. I didn't expect any results other than Brendan's being ordered to serve out his original sentence.

The judge sent him back to Trinity House to serve his time. Then the judge gave an order that my expenses for the Nenagh and Waterford sessions be paid. I was grateful for the assistance.

Brendan later phoned me to ask me whether I was coming up to a case conference. I told him I had been asked to go and I drove up early on the morning of the conference. I think it was the end of March 1990. I took his grandmother, Mary Quinn, and his sister, Ann Marie, with me.

While Mary Quinn and Ann Marie were visiting Brendan, I had a chance to talk to some staff members about him. One of them told me about an alarming incident.

Brendan had been coming back from a weekend pass, and had been waiting some minutes for a car to pick him up at the railway station in Dublin. He later said that while he was sitting there, a train was passing, and he saw a cat run out in front of it and get its head cut off. According to Brendan, there was blood everywhere. Apparently he considered it a very funny story and started grinning uncontrollably as he told it.

5

Anti-psychotic Drugs

JJ Muggivan

When Tony first got me involved in the story of Brendan O'Donnell, I intended to write a very basic account of his life and attempt to find out what had brought him to do what he did. I started with some assumptions that problems of the kind Brendan had arise somehow within the family and spiral out of control. However, as Tony and I gathered more information throughout the years, I came to believe that the story was far more complex.

When I first met Brendan, I did not know a lot about his psychological problems. In later years, I read the impressions of him given by Dr Gerry O'Neill during the trial. In my opinion, the Brendan O'Donnell I knew bears close resemblance to the Brendan O'Donnell described by Dr O'Neill.

Dr O'Neill, a visiting consultant at Trinity House, examined Brendan when he had been there a few weeks. In all, Dr O'Neill saw him seven times, more than he had

ever seen any other boy there. The meetings took place
between 1988 and 1990. At the first meeting, he found a
gentle, quiet, withdrawn boy who had been bullied and
who had difficulties coping with the Dublin boys. The
staff at Trinity House had taken steps to deal with the
bullying and the situation had improved.

Dr O'Neill found Brendan open and direct and easy to
talk to. He admitted his difficulties at school and how
hard he found the work. His schoolmates nicknamed him
'Hitman' because of his obvious interest in guns. This had
started when he went clay-pigeon shooting with his uncle
in England and had got to the point that he seemed to
know every house in his area that had a gun. The early
loss of his mother, with whom he had an over-close
relationship, appeared to have worsened his problems.
Although he said at first that he was pleased that his
father had re-married, he later asserted vehemently that
he felt pushed aside when his stepmother came into the
family and that his father took little notice of him.

Given three wishes, Brendan said that his were that his
mother had not died, that he could go home again and
that he would not use the shotgun again. He said that the
three people closest to him were his dead mother, his
youngest brother, Aidan, and his sister, Ann Marie. She
had been like a second mother to him; on one occasion she
had persuaded him to hand over a gun to the guards following an incident when he had fired a gun at a door that
a guard had walked through.

Dr O'Neill formed the view that Brendan was losing
touch with reality and was potentially psychotic. A second
psychiatric opinion endorsed this view. He believed that
Brendan presented an element of danger to society and
appeared to have no scruples about killing or shooting
people for revenge, especially if it were against other

Trinity House prisoners or for the IRA. Brendan seemed to be under the delusion that he was involved with the IRA, that the IRA were trying to rescue him from Trinity House and were sending him coded messages through the radio, calling him Rambo.

Dr O'Neill's recommendation was that Brendan should be kept in a secure setting for some time, and treated by adult psychiatric services. Brendan would have to agree to this, however, and he was not enthusiastic about moving to a small residential community under adult care. It was Dr O'Neill's opinion that a good environment, not medication, was more likely to provide a solution to Brendan's problems. However, he was not accepted for a place at a suitable facility in Galway, which is how he ended up in Trinity House. He transferred briefly to a smaller institution in Clonmel, but he escaped from there and was returned to Trinity House.

Brendan's father stated to a news reporter on one occasion that he felt as if he had been bringing Brendan to psychiatrists all of his life. To some extent, this is true. Michael Pat O'Donnell's son might not have been helped but the trips to doctors and to institutions left the kind of a record we rarely get on individuals like Brendan.

Thus, Brendan's story requires an examination of his family life experience, but also his experience of mental-health care. The record is full of information that he was injured by *both* his family life experience and the health care he received. As I play my part in the telling of his story, I am guided by information gathered from both of these life experiences.

Because of what I discovered in the course of my work, I have changed my mind many times about Brendan's worsening mental-health problems and how they brought him to act as he did.

I have often asked Tony what kind of teenager arrived in his home on 16 February 1989. His contribution to this account is his answer. Working backwards, and after I had obtained large quantities of information, I asked what kind of mental-health care Brendan was receiving when he ran away from Trinity House and before he arrived at my brother's house.

Prior to running away from Trinity House, Brendan had, in fact, been on heavy anti-psychotic medication. In June 1988, Dr O'Neill had judged him to be psychotic and a certain danger to society. Apparently at that time, Brendan was suffering delusions about involvement with the IRA, who he believed were trying to rescue him from the detention centre. He told Dr O'Neill that the IRA called him 'Rambo' and sent him coded messages through the radio. Brendan was also seen by Dr Charles Smith who, like Dr O'Neill, suspected psychosis. Anti-psychotic treatment was prescribed for the then fourteen-year-old boy, and when the delusions appeared to fade, the doctors believed their diagnosis to have been correct, and Brendan continued on the treatment.

There is evidence that some anti-psychotic drugs can actually create a dependence which is, in itself, a disease, the symptoms of which would include a huge indifference, fever, sweating and heart problems. According to Dr Peter Breggin, author of *Toxic Psychiatry*, in severe cases, these can result in 'delirium, coma, and death'. Moreover, patients who apparently make a complete recovery might, years later, become unexpectedly ill again. Dr Breggin writes:

The profession of psychiatry now agrees that the drug-induced neurological disorders do become permanent in a large percentage of patients. In addition, there is growing incontrovertible evidence that permanent psychosis and dementia also are frequent outcomes. . . .

When children are given anti-psychotic drugs, there is a danger that after several months of treatment, they will become very anxious, thus requiring larger doses of the medication. And any patients attempting to come off the medication would require support from trained professionals.

It is possible that when Brendan did not return to Trinity House, and did not receive any medication or treatment at either Ballinasloe or Galway, he was, in fact, suffering sudden withdrawal. This might have had the effect of worsening the original psychotic symptoms and causing him anxiety and anguish.

Brendan's record calls for an examination of how, when, and why his symptoms developed.

6

Probation Revoked

Tony Muggivan

———————

I told JJ about my conversation with the administrator at Trinity House. I also told him about how I was always confused at Brendan's unusual habit of laughing and giggling at things that weren't funny. The following is a report JJ sent to me after I talked to him.

On 12/18/1989 [18 December 1989], ten months after Brendan O'Donnell arrived at the Muggivan home, and after he had his probation revoked . . . I told my brother by letter that he had signs of serious emotional disturbance. I told him that the reported history of violence was most important in understanding him.

I advised Tony that care should be taken that he be guarded from endangering himself or others and I told him that the reported history of sexual and physical abuse placed him at high risk of becoming an abuser himself. I suggested that this may have already begun to occur. I said the most likely candidates for suicide attempts are the offspring of parents who have committed suicide or made suicide attempts.

I responded to the reports of killing animals and suggested that this was a very serious indicator of problems. I advised Tony not to leave Brendan around children, unsupervised, until he had been cleared by a qualified mental-health professional. I recommended that the best treatment plan for Brendan would be institutional care. I proposed that Brendan not be released until he no longer needed external controls to manage his anger, impulsiveness, and potential for violence.

I advised that Brendan's depression be addressed and that he not be released until this was done and until he had developed clear life goals being actively pursued in a realistic way. I advised that Brendan not be released until he had demonstrated being able to leave institutional care into someone's supervision to whom he would be responsible for a fairly long period of time. I warned Tony that I was not for taking any chances until there would be clear signs that Brendan would be unlikely to harm himself or others.

I sent my brother material from the Diagnostic and Statistical Manual (DSM-III-R) of the American Psychiatric Association (APA), and advised him not to share the material with Brendan since he was capable of using it for manipulation purposes rather than for therapeutic purposes. The material I sent included the diagnoses for Conduct Disorder, Under-socialized, Aggressive, and Major Depressive Disorder. It was clear at the time that Brendan was suffering from, at least, both of these disorders as described in DSM-III-R. (JJ Muggivan)

I asked an administrator at Trinity House why Brendan had a bandage on his left wrist. His said that Brendan had cut his wrist, in the administrator's presence, after getting upset.

We talked for some time. He told me that he had never wanted to take Brendan into Trinity House in the first place as he was too young for that detention centre.

He was allowed out on weekend passes in 1990, but he would run away. Once, he went to his father's house, when he should have been back in Trinity House. The Killaloe guards phoned me to go with them to talk to him. They were afraid he would set fire to his father's house or injure himself.

When we got there, he was gone. Before we left, his stepmother came home and she complained to the senior officer, saying that she had a young child and was concerned for his safety. Everyone was afraid.

Brendan would always phone and tell me he was tired of running and wanted to go back. I would arrange for him to be picked up as he never wanted the guards to take him. When I pushed him to tell me why, he laughed and told me that they could do what they liked with you when they got you in. He said that if he got a chance, he would do a guard in.

I heard that he was mistreated by a guard in Galway and, from what I heard — from others as well as Brendan — I have no reason to doubt what he told me. Because of one guard's actions, another could have been shot.

After the last time Brendan ran away while on a weekend pass, I heard that he had been sent to Spike Island in Cork. This is an island in Cork harbour which has a prison for adults.

In the nineteenth century, when Ireland was under British rule, Spike Island was home to a barracks for British soldiers. However, with the treaty of 1921, which concluded the 1916–21 war for Irish independence, the island was transferred over to the new Irish Government. The buildings were transformed into a prison.

Not long after Brendan's arrival there, some inmates put drugs in his drink, causing him to fall asleep. They then burned his feet in boiling water.

After this incident, he made the most serious attempt on his own life. He had an inmate cut his wrist to the bone while he held a rag in his mouth to keep himself from screaming. He was found and taken to a doctor before he could bleed to death.

I heard that, a short time later, he was transferred to St Vincent's Hospital in Dublin. When his wrist was cut, the tendons were also cut. The injury required extensive surgery to repair both the wound and the tendons.

While at St Vincent's Hospital, Brendan tried to rip out the stitches from his wrist. He was placed on continual suicide watch. When he was considered safe to move, he was transferred to Dundrum Mental Hospital — a hospital for the criminally insane. At this time, he was just over sixteen years of age.

Between his stay at St Vincent's and his transfer to Dundrum, I believe he spent some time in Wheatfield Prison. I remember driving to Dublin to see him with my sister-in-law, Josephine O'Brien, and being told that he had been moved.

We stopped in Kildare on our way to Dublin and Josephine brought some clothes for him. When we arrived at Wheatfield Prison, we were made to wait several hours before being told that he was not there but was in the city. We left the clothes for him and drove home to Mountshannon.

Brendan later told me that he was in hospital at the time because he had been beaten up by an inmate.

When my brother, JJ, came over on holidays in the summer of 1990, I brought him to Dundrum. Previously, Kevin Brennan, who was on the staff at Trinity House, had asked me to try to get background family information on Brendan, as no one in Dublin seemed to know anything about his early life.

I called JJ and he advised me to call Joe Carney to do a social history and send it to Kevin Brennan.

I felt bad about having bothered Joe Carney so much over the previous year, and having taken up so much of his time, so I decided to try to get as much history as I could myself. I talked to as many people as I could.

I had plenty of time to talk to his sister and grand-mother because of driving to Dublin with them. They gave me a lot of information.

I wrote it all down and sent it to Kevin Brennan.

Since then, JJ has done a more detailed childhood history of Brendan, which he writes about in the following chapters.

7

Troubled Early Life
JJ Muggivan

My brother, Tony, and Brendan's sister, Ann Marie, helped me to compile the following history of Brendan's early life. My relationship with Brendan was through my brother. I met him only twice — first during his first stay at Dundrum and, later, after he had been released, at a festival in Scarriff, County Clare.

In preparing this history, I reviewed published reports of the trial testimony. I interviewed his grandmother, his sister, and Brendan himself. I also interviewed people who knew him and his family, and I reviewed records produced by school personnel and mental-health professionals.

Important information was provided to me by one local in particular, who has known the family almost from the time of Brendan's parents' marriage until the present.

Brendan was born in Cregg House, which is about one mile from Whitegate, about three miles from Mountshannon, and about two miles from the border between Clare and Galway. Whitegate and Mountshannon are small villages in east Clare, located close to Lough Derg, a lake on the River Shannon. They are the last two villages in Clare before entering Galway on the road leading north from Killaloe to Portumna.

There are two roads from Mountshannon to the Galway border, one of which runs through Whitegate. The other one runs about one mile on the northwest side of the village of Whitegate. There is a third road through the mountains into Woodford in County Galway, but it is rarely used.

Cregg House is on the road running on the northwest side of the village of Whitegate.

At the time of his parents' marriage, Brendan's father lived in Cregg House and his mother lived in Eyrecourt, County Galway, with her mother, Mary Quinn, and her father. Whitegate and Eyrecourt are about twenty-seven miles apart.

The mother's maiden name was Margaret Quinn and she was about twenty-three years old at the time of her marriage. Brendan's father, Michael Pat O'Donnell, was about three years older. They were married on 31 July 1969.

Mary Quinn described her daughter as a normal, happy child. As a teenager, she liked to dance and would cycle miles to dances in the villages and towns around Eyrecourt. Mary Quinn's description of her daughter suggests nothing unusual in her childhood, adolescence, or young adulthood.

Margaret had one brother and one sister. She got on well with them, especially the brother who was younger than her by thirteen years.

Margaret and Michael Pat's first-born child, and Brendan's only sister, Ann Marie, was born on 22 July 1970. Brendan's older brother was born just over two years later in November 1972. Brendan was the third child and was born a year and four months after his older brother, on 24 March 1974. He was about eight years and five months old when the fourth child was born in the summer of 1982.

Ann Marie described Brendan as a happy infant who did not begin to show signs of difficulty until shortly before starting school. However, she described him as a 'colicky' baby, saying that he was an infant who cried a lot and was difficult to put to sleep.

With the exception of recalling that Brendan was a 'colicky' baby, Ann Marie's first recollection of signs of problems was her memory of seeing him crying in the morning at having to go to school and wanting his mother to be with him all the time. He would not go to school unless accompanied by his mother. He began to refuse to sleep in his own bed, wanting, instead, to have his mother sleep with him.

Brendan's father worked for the Clare County Council and continues to work there to this day. Mary Quinn and Ann Marie described Michael Pat O'Donnell as a perfectionist who had to have everything done his way. From early on, the maternal grandparents and Ann Marie blamed Michael Pat for Brendan's emerging problems. They related Brendan's problems to what they described as his father's use of 'excessive discipline'.

Ann Marie and Brendan reported that their father emphasised cleanliness to a fault. Ann Marie reported that she has habits of cleanliness today which come from her father's demands.

One local who knew the family well claims that reports of excessive physical discipline by Michael Pat were exaggerated and that she never saw marks on Brendan and never heard of complaints of serious beatings.

This person believes that the mother gave exaggerated accounts of beatings and that she had a significant amount of control over family discipline.

Regarding reports of physical punishment or mistreatment of his son, *The Irish Times* gave the following report on 4 February 1996:

> Meanwhile, O'Donnell's father, Michael Pat — alleged during the trial to have physically mistreated his son — denied yesterday that he had brutalized him and said he would never forgive him.

The above accounts are supported by an account given to the *Clare Champion* newspaper by one of Brendan's teachers, Mr Jim Collins. Mr Collins reported that during the time he knew Brendan, he never saw signs of physical beatings of any kind.

The one local I spoke to who was most familiar with the O'Donnell family after the family had moved from Cregg Wood to the village of Whitegate told me that Michael Pat was a father who always took good physical care of his children. He made sure they always received needed medical care, had good clothes to wear, and had good food.

Brendan Muggivan confirmed much of the foregoing. He told me that when Brendan O'Donnell attended Mountshannon School, he was always well dressed and that other pupils would sometimes be envious of the lunches he brought to school, especially such food items as biscuits. This was after the mother's death and when Ann Marie now lived at home with her father and the two older brothers.

It seems that Ann Marie and her father took good care of the two boys. However, Ann Marie believes that Michael Pat had become disillusioned with Brendan and was ready to leave his discipline to others.

Reports in some newspapers suggested that Michael Pat had a problem with drinking. Locals told me that he did not have a drinking problem. One local told me that when the children were young, he would go to the pub only on a weekend night and have only a couple, or a few, beers on any given occasion.

She said that she has never seen him drunk at any time in the twenty-five to thirty years she has known him. Several locals gave me similar accounts of moderate drinking habits.

There was agreement between all those interviewed that Michael Pat was a perfectionist about cleanliness. Ann Marie and her grandmother reported that the father would get very angry when the children got their shoes, their clothes, or themselves dirty or soiled.

They both reported that the mother was under great pressure to keep them clean and keep them dressed in clean clothes.

Mary Quinn and Ann Marie reported that the father seemed to favour the older brother over Brendan.

When Margaret visited her mother's house she would, according to Mary Quinn, bring a change of clothes for the children, so that, when the father would visit, they would all be dressed in clean clothes. Neatness was strictly imposed, according to Mary Quinn.

I obtained descriptions of Margaret's illnesses from people who knew her, rather than from mental-health professionals. 'Depression' was the most common description used by her friends and family members.

Ann Marie does not recall her mother being significantly depressed until Brendan began showing problems related to going to school. However, the record shows that both Brendan and his mother were showing signs of serious problems before he started school, with Brendan's problems starting at least by the age of three.

The mother's depression was attributed to her difficult relationship with her husband. The account given by Mary Quinn and Ann Marie suggests that Margaret developed her depression either shortly before or shortly after Brendan's birth. However, at least one friend reported that Margaret had signs of depression even before her marriage, and that she frequently complained of physical symptoms.

A local woman told me that Margaret complained of illnesses for as long as she knew her. She told me that she remembers occasions when she would call Michael Pat at work to come home and take her to the doctor and that Michael Pat would always rush home when called.

Other parents reported that Margaret was always fearful of her children getting hurt, or catching a cold. Her fears for her children's safety and health caused her to keep them close to her at all times.

The local woman told me that Margaret was finicky about the children and that whenever they got involved in conflicts with local children, she would immediately engage in the conflict on the side of her children.

The local woman remembers that Margaret was always present while the children played outside, either standing at the door or looking out the window.

The mother's over-protectiveness appears to have been a problem from very early on. I spoke to a number of locals who recalled Brendan's mother not allowing visitors to drive their cars close to the home in the evening time in order not to waken the children. They reported that, at a certain set time, radios and televisions had to be turned off for the same reason.

This anxiety about disturbing the children's rest was evident before the family moved to the village of Whitegate — when Brendan was under two years of age.

It is not known for certain how long Margaret O'Donnell was taking prescription medication, but it appears that she may have been taking medication throughout all of Brendan's life — and possibly before he was born. People who knew her when she was younger reported that she complained of mostly physical symptoms, even from before her marriage.

Triptasol and Valium are the two medicines mentioned in the records as having been prescribed for Margaret.

When Brendan was about five-and-a half years old, Ann Marie, who was about nine at the time, went to live with her grandmother in Eyrecourt, County Galway. She continued to see her mother, her two brothers and her father during their weekend visits to her grandmother's home in Eyrecourt.

Margaret was in and out of hospital. When she came with her two sons to visit her mother and Ann Marie, she would seem severely depressed. She was forgetful. She always looked tired. The children would call her and she appeared not to hear them and would not answer. She spent most of her time in bed. Ann Marie said she made numerous suicide attempts.

During one visit, Mary Quinn gave Margaret some eggs to take home with her. Mary Quinn said that when she was handing her daughter the eggs, if she had put them in her outstretched hands, they would have dropped to the floor. Her daughter walked around in a daze much of the time, giving the appearance of sleepwalking. She appeared oblivious to what was happening around her.

Mary Quinn attributed her daughter's unhappiness, her behaviour and her depression to her bad marriage.

A local described an experience she had with Margaret after the youngest child was born. Brendan was about nine years old. When Margaret came home from the hospital with the baby, the woman went to her house with a gift for the new baby. When she knocked at the door, Margaret looked out the window and told her she couldn't come in because the baby had a cold and she didn't want to risk exposing him to germs.

About the same time, Margaret began going to a local's house in the evening time to watch one of her favourite television shows, *Dallas*. After a few weeks, the woman asked her what was wrong with her own television. Margaret told her that Brendan had destroyed it during a temper tantrum and that he had also destroyed much of her furniture.

An expert who testified at Brendan's trial made reference to a medical record suggesting that at least one doctor had concerns that Margaret had signs of schizophrenia.

The O'Donnell family lived in Cregg House for about six years after the marriage, and moved to the village of Whitegate when Brendan was about two years old. Ann Marie left the family home to live with her grandmother in Eyrecourt, County Galway, when Brendan was about five. Her memory of Brendan refusing to go to school suggests that she left the family home some time after he started attending school.

As psychiatrist Dr Michael Ledwith saw Brendan and his parents many times from 1978 to 1985, his trial testimony is the best record of Brendan's early life. According to that testimony, Brendan had displayed severe behavioural problems from as young as four years of age.

Dr Ledwith first met the O'Donnells on 17 February 1978. Brendan had been referred to his assessment clinic by the public health services. At the time, Michael Pat O'Donnell was thirty-four, and Margaret was thirty-one. Margaret had taken an overdose the previous year and had been seen by a psychiatrist at the local regional hospital but she had not continued to attend.

When I interviewed him years later in Dundrum, Brendan gave me a detailed description of his mother's suicide attempt. He told me that she had taken an overdose of pills and had drunk a half bottle of whisky. He confirmed that when his mother had fallen, she had hit her nose on a cabinet, causing her to bleed profusely.

Dr Ledwith recorded that Brendan had been 8lb 4oz at birth, that he had smiled at six months, and had walked at sixteen months. However, his mother went on to tell the doctor of attacks Brendan would get, when he would turn very pale. She said that this happened at times of tension when he was reprimanded for doing something wrong and was physically punished. She said that she didn't know how else to correct him.

We do not know whether Brendan developed the symptoms of turning pale and getting 'attacks' before or after witnessing his mother's suicide attempt. However, it seems that the symptoms developed after the attempt.

Dr Ledwith told Michael Pat and Margaret that physical punishment was not an appropriate response to Brendan's behavioural problems.

Margaret O'Donnell complained to the doctor that she herself was treated like a servant by her husband and that he displayed no affection towards his children. Dr Ledwith saw that she had great difficulty in coping, and was concerned about the family as a whole. Aware that they needed his support and that of the social services, he saw the family as a whole on nine separate occasions up to 1979.

His second meeting with Brendan was on 4 August 1978, when Margaret told him that Brendan was sometimes aggressive and needed a lot of love. Six months later, on 2 February 1979, Dr Ledwith noted that Brendan was hallucinating at night. He prescribed Valium to help the child to sleep and to get over his night terrors. Dr Ledwith said at Brendan's trial that this was the practice in the late 1970s. However, he acknowledged that, by the time of the trial, it had ceased to be common practice.

Brendan again attended Dr Ledwith on 6 April and 27 April of the same year. Margaret told the doctor that there had been no improvement and that Brendan would not stay in school or settle at night. She was having difficulty in coping with all her children and expressed a desire to have a break for a while. Dr Ledwith found Brendan to be pleasant and cooperative with him but because the child was still bed-wetting at night, wetting his trousers during the day and demonstrating other behavioural problems, he recommended a psychiatric assessment and put him on a new drug, now usually used in the treatment of adults.

When Dr Ledwith saw Margaret O'Donnell again, on 11 May 1979, he recorded that there were major problems in the family. However, Margaret told him that her son was a little better although still moody, with bouts of whingeing. She said that she had no problems with Brendan when he was on his own with her, but that the problems related to difficulties with Michael Pat. She told the doctor that she was 'at the end of her tether'. Dr Ledwith then saw Brendan and recorded that he was happy and playing at a level appropriate to his age.

However, the doctor was becoming increasingly concerned about the situation in the family. He proposed that a social worker visit the family home and suggested that Margaret be placed in short-term care where she might receive treatment.

On 1 June 1979, Margaret told Dr Ledwith that Brendan was improving, was sleeping well and was whingeing less. He still had a poor relationship with his sister and brother, but he had been attending school. However, he had a very poor appetite. Dr Ledwith prescribed Triptasol — a vitamin preparation to help Brendan's appetite.

At this stage, Margaret O'Donnell was anxious that she herself be hospitalised and that the children be in care if that occurred. She told Dr Ledwith that her husband didn't care about her emotional problems.

Brendan was referred for psychological assessment on 11 June. The report described him as a little boy of pale complexion with fair curly hair. His mother was with him for the assessment and he would not separate from her. He held his finger in his mouth and scratched his back with his right hand and would often twist about in the chair. He spoke quietly but clearly. Tests indicated that his present functioning was a little below average. It was recommended that he attend for psychiatric review and it was stated that he would benefit from school. Brendan was five years old at the time.

A month later, on 6 July 1979, Margaret told Dr Ledwith that Brendan was 'back to square one' and that he had many fears and worries. Brendan had told her that there were worms coming out of his ears and he was also afraid of animals and said that he saw them in his food. Moreover, he had fits of laughter for no apparent reason. Once again, Margaret expressed the opinion that her husband was at the root of the family's problems.

A social-work report from 1979, based on an interview with Margaret O'Donnell, spoke of Michael Pat's having a poor relationship with his children and inconsistent treatment of them. Margaret was described in this report as a nervous, anxious person who was taking tablets for her nerves and had tried to commit suicide. She had described her children as 'nervous wrecks' who were 'needled' by their father and could not sleep properly.

In August 1979, the O'Donnells arranged an emergency appointment with Dr Ledwith. Margaret was very anxious to get treatment for her own problems, and Michael Pat had agreed to her going into a psychiatric hospital. The social services were apparently trying to organise short-term care for the children. Margaret told the doctor that Brendan was a bit better but still wanted to be with her in bed at night.

Dr Ledwith did not see Brendan again.

In March 1985, when he was almost eleven years old, Brendan was accompanied by his father to see a psychiatrist in Bawnmore. Margaret O'Donnell had died in January 1984, and their youngest son was in England. Michael Pat told the psychiatrist that none of his children were getting on at school, and he hoped to transfer Brendan to Mountshannon national school. He did not report any difficulties with Brendan at home and said he was very helpful around the house.

The psychologist reported that Brendan was alert and co-operative and had said that he liked school and had forgotten his mother.

A number of psychological tests were carried out on Brendan at this time and his intelligence functioning was found to be borderline range between mild mental handicap and low average. Another test showed that he had a mental age of 7–8 and he had a word recognition range of 8.7 years. The report recommended a psychiatric appointment and a conference discussion with a social worker involved with the family.

* * *

In the 1970s, Valium was widely prescribed for all kinds of symptoms, especially the symptoms of depression and anxiety. At the time, it was not known that this was a highly addictive drug, every bit as addictive as alcohol.

Having complained of severe emotional distress for a long period of time, Margaret O'Donnell was a very likely candidate for medication with Valium. And as her symptoms were severe, she was most likely to be administered the drug in higher and higher doses.

As Margaret O'Donnell took Valium or a similar drug as a medicine for her symptoms for such a long period of time, it is useful to note what has since been written about its effects and its similarity to alcohol. The DSM-IV-TR (Diagnostic and Statistical Manual of Mental Disorders) is the most widely used psychiatric reference in the world. It lists and identifies the symptoms of a total of fifteen disorders associated with sedative, hypnotic and anxiolytic medication such as Valium (pp 284–5). It describes these drugs as follows:

> Like alcohol, these agents are brain depressants and can produce similar substance-induced and substance-use disorders. At high doses sedatives, hypnotics and anxiolytics can be lethal, particularly when mixed with alcohol.

The DSM goes on to describe how these drugs can cause significant changes in behaviour and may be accompanied by 'slurred speech, an unsteady gait, nystagmus, memory or attentional problems, levels of incoordination that can interefere with driving abilities and with performing usual activities to the point of causing falls or automobile accidents, and stupor or coma.'

Mary Quinn's description of her daughter's appearance during visits is noteworthy in this respect. She said that her daughter slept all the time, would appear not to hear her children when they called, and walked around in a daze. I believe that what she was observing was not

74

clinical depression, but sedation from Valium. In other words, her daughter was showing signs similar to signs one would see in someone who is drunk.

Drugs such as Valium are addictive and can be lethal. The DSM-IV-TR states that 'very significant levels of physiological dependence, marked by both tolerance and withdrawal, can develop to the [drugs] . . . antisocial behaviour and antisocial personality disorder are associated with sedative, hypnotic or anxiolytic dependence and abuse'.

Addiction can occur within two to four weeks, and prolonged use of Valium can cause an intensification of the symptoms causing its use. In other words, for the first few days of drinking, symptoms of anxiety and depression can lessen in intensity. However, after drinking for a longer period of time, anxiety and depression can worsen. This increase and worsening of depression and anxiety symptoms can now cause an individual to increase consumption of what caused relaxation at the beginning.

Withdrawal from use can intensify the symptoms even more. The DSM-IV-TR describes the problem of withdrawal as follows:

> The withdrawal syndrome produced by substances in this class may be characterized by the development of a delirium that can be life threatening. There may be evidence of tolerance and withdrawal in the absence of a diagnosis of Substance Dependence in an individual who has abruptly discontinued benzodiazepines [Valium] that were taken for long periods of time at prescribed and therapeutic doses.

When the anxiety worsened — now because of the medication — medicine, such as Valium, was usually increased, making the anxiety worse.

Continued use of this medication at high levels can cause more than an increase or intensification in anxiety or depression symptoms, however:

The minor tranquilizers can produce paradoxical reactions — acute agitation, confusion, disorientation, anxiety, and aggression — especially in children . . . reactions such as stimulation, agitation, rage, increased muscle spasticity, sleep disturbances, hallucinations and other adverse behavioral effects may occur in rare instances and in random fashion. . . . (Breggin, *Toxic Psychiatry*)

It should be noted that Margaret's medical record was cited during the trial as containing a suggestion that she had psychotic symptoms (schizophrenia). The DSM-IV-TR writes of the connection between drugs such as Valium and psychotic symptoms and the dangers of withdrawal without medical care:

In severe withdrawal, visual, tactile or auditory hallucinations or illusions can occur . . . the longer the substance has been taken and the higher the dosages used the more likely it is that there will be severe withdrawal.

The possibility that Margaret O'Donnell became suicidal because of her medication cannot be ruled out either. According to the DSM-IV-TR, the use of these drugs can lead to many problems, including attempted and completed sucides:

Some data indicate that the disinhibiting effects of these agents can, like alcohol, actually contribute to overly aggressive behavior, with subsequent interpersonal and legal problems. Intense or repeated sedative, hypnotic or anxiolytic intoxication may be associated with severe depression that, although temporary, can be intense enough to lead to suicide attempts and completed suicides (p. 289).

I believe that Margaret was heavily medicated and addicted to Valium. This addiction profoundly affected her life. Most importantly, it profoundly affected the life of her son, Brendan. The evidence that he was addicted in the womb is compelling, both from the history and the nature of his lifelong symptoms.

Margaret and Brendan O'Donnell were treated in the 1970s and 1980s. However, newer guidelines for the appropriate use of minor tranquillisers, such as Valium, are now in effect.

8

After His Mother's Death

JJ Muggivan

After her mother's death, Ann Marie returned to Whitegate to live with her father and two of her brothers. The youngest brother, who was seventeen months old when his mother died, was taken to England to be raised by an aunt.

Brendan continued to attend school in Whitegate. For some time after his mother's death, Brendan was found several times at her grave. He would either ride his bicycle or walk the two miles from his home in Whitegate to Clonrush graveyard.

Now that Ann Marie had moved back to Whitegate, she had an opportunity to get to know her brother well. She had been separated from him for about seven years and knew him only from visits back and forth between Whitegate and Eyrecourt.

Shortly after his mother died, Brendan began to believe that she had managed to find enough medicine in the hospital to kill herself. He developed the theory that his mother would steal medicine from the nurse's tray as the nurse was taking the medicine around to each patient.

Eventually, according to his theory, his mother had enough medicine to kill herself from an overdose, and that she did. Brendan repeated this theory to me in my interview with him at Dundrum in 1989.

Ann Marie noticed the continuing grief in Brendan over his mother's death. She noticed that when something went wrong, he would go to her grave and lie on it, sometimes into the night.

She also noticed some strange behaviours she had not previously seen. For a lengthy period of time, Brendan had been asking her to save old bread and bread crumbs for him. He explained that he had a pet fox out in the fields across from where they lived, and that he needed the bread to feed it.

Ann Marie complied with his demands and would save the bread and bread crumbs for him. At intervals, Brendan would put the bread and crumbs in his pockets and leave the house to go to feed the fox.

Ann Marie became curious about the pet fox and wondered about her brother's relationship with it. She had trouble believing that a child could get close enough to a wild fox to make it into a pet.

One day, she asked if she could go with him to feed the fox. He brought her with him. When they arrived at the place where he had reported having the pet fox, Brendan got down on his knees and began calling to the fox to come out of the bushes. He took the bread out of his pocket and placed it on the ground in front of him.

After a while calling, he said to Ann Marie, 'Isn't he a lovely fox?'

Ann Marie responded, 'I can't see a fox at all', and recalled that 'there was never a fox around anywhere'. It was clear to her, however, that the fox was very real to her brother.

Brendan got upset when his sister was unable to see the fox but he finally accepted that, indeed, she could not see it. He then asked her not to tell his friends that she had not seen his fox as they might believe what she said rather than what he was saying. Ann Marie told him she would not tell his friends anything about the fox.

She noticed many other unusual behaviours. One day, he was riding his bicycle by the post office in Whitegate and got a bad fall. He broke his leg in two places. When people came to give him assistance, he showed no signs of pain or distress.

Instead, he was laughing. His leg was put in a cast and he was advised to be careful until the leg was ready for the cast to be taken off. He ignored the warnings and rode his bike regularly until the cast was eventually removed.

The year following his mother's death, Brendan was transferred from Whitegate school to Mountshannon school. He attended Mountshannon school from 4 April 1985 to 30 June 1987, riding his bicycle the three to four miles from his home to the school, together with his older brother, David. The principal of Mountshannon school was Jim Collins and he gave evidence at Brendan's trial to the effect that Brendan was 'the most disturbed child I would have had'.

Jim Collins told the court that when Brendan first arrived at the school he was a quite polite child and showed no signs of behavioural problems. It was clear to him though that Brendan had taken his mother's death badly. He did not make close friends and seemed to rely on his brother a lot. He also seemed to be quite suspicious of everyone and watched the teachers closely while they were supervising play-time.

Brendan was behind the rest of his class with his school work, and the principal said in court that he would have considered him to be a suitable candidate for remedial work.

Jim Collins recalled that around March and April 1987, Brendan began to be absent from school, sometimes not turning up at all, and on two occasions arriving only to disappear before school started. On the first of these occasions, the principal had eventually found his pupil after a search, and had persuaded him to return to the school, but Brendan had refused to go into the building. He had agreed to work in the school garden, however.

Shortly afterwards, an agreement was reached between the school and the O'Donnells that Brendan would continue to attend until his Confirmation in June 1987. He remained on after his Confirmation, in order to captain the school hurling team in the primary schools' final. Brendan scored a number of goals, and the school won the final that year.

Jim Collins said in testimony that he believed his pupil had acquired reading and writing skills and could read a newspaper and write ordinary letters.

In the summer of 1990, Tony asked me to go with him to visit Brendan in the Central Mental Hospital in Dundrum in Dublin. At the time, I did not know about the opinions of Doctors Gerry O'Neill and Charles Smith. Dr Smith had seen Brendan in 1990 after his transfer from Spike Island to the Central Mental Hospital. Brendan had a mutilated left arm, and Dr Smith testified that self-injuries such as Brendan's were common among people with personality disorders.

I spoke to Brendan for twenty minutes, and later made a written record of our discussion. In the course of our conversation, Brendan told me that his father had never been able to show affection for him and was unable to engage with him in any kind of intimate or personal conversation. According to Brendan, when his father had paid a visit recently, their only discussion had been about the weather.

In sharp contrast to what Brendan described as extreme emotional estrangement from his father was the relationship he told me had existed with his mother. He said that he had been very close to her, and I saw numerous signs that he had not fully mourned her loss. He told me of visits he had made to her grave since her death, and I could see clear signs of unresolved grief questions, particularly the perception that his mother was a tragic figure, unloved and uncared for by her husband.

When Brendan and I discussed his attempted suicide, it was clear that he had intended it to result in death. From my professional knowledge and experience, I could see that it had been a classic adolescent attempt with typical features. Brendan did not see himself as having control over his body, his mind or his life. As a result, he seemed to be fed with an angry desire to end what he believed was controlled and owned by others. Imagined satisfaction was available to him by the belief that he could at least control his death and thereby arouse a sense of grief in those to whom he wished to be close.

As Brendan had still not reconciled his conflicted feelings over the death of his mother and his inability to communicate with his father, and as he had not increased personal control over his own decision-making power concerning his destiny, I felt it was distinctly possible that he would attempt suicide again.

I also saw a possibility that his anger, frustration and other pent-up feelings might result in anti-social behaviour if they were not addressed in appropriate psychotherapy.

It seemed to me to be important that Brendan be given the opportunity to participate in a reasonably normal adolescent environment. He told me that the jacket he was wearing belonged to a young man with whom he had developed a friendship. This man had, reportedly, been incarcerated for killing a number of people in a fit of rage. In this environment of adults, who were clearly not models for social growth and development, Brendan was easy, vulnerable prey to the needs of those around him.

My overall impression was that Brendan was in an extremely confused emotional state and highly susceptible to influence from any adult. Because of his failure to form a strong attachment with an authority or father figure, it seemed likely that he would form relationships which would support his anger towards such figures. Deprived as he was of opportunities to socialise with peers of the opposite sex, he would not be able to form a real relationship which might have aroused and nurtured more positive feelings.

I had heard the reports that Brendan had been sexually abused and felt that if these reports were true, they could be causing serious sexual confusion at that crucial stage in his development.

Brendan's prolonged depression and the absence of nurturing relationships had apparently given rise to the development of an aggressive conduct disorder which, it seemed to me, was likely to worsen without an appropriate treatment plan. I felt that Brendan would have benefited from such a plan. He came across as intelligent, very verbal and articulate, and he was capable of a good deal of insight when engaged in a relaxing conversation. I could see that he was highly manipulative in his relationships, but my overall impressions were that his manipulative tactics were fairly obvious, easy to identify, and could have been readily bypassed or confronted in therapy.

Brendan was due to be released the following March, at which time he would, in effect be asked to assume control. I believed that he needed treatment prior to that release and that the process of his taking control over his life needed to be initiated immediately.

Following our visit with Brendan in the Central Mental Hospital, Tony and I had a conversation with Super-intendent Con McCarthy outside Scariff garda station. The superintendent's concern at the time was that nothing was being done for Brendan while he was in prison, and that, consequently, he was likely to come out worse than when he had gone in. Con McCarthy said that he was having nightmares that Brendan would, later on, go into the home of some old person who might be living alone and kill them. People who live in the country are uniquely vulnerable to criminal activity. It could be days before a crime against someone living alone might be discovered.

The superintendent couldn't understand how people who were not trained in psychology could see the problem before them, yet the professionals did not seem to be doing anything. I said I would write a report of my assessment of Brendan and send it to Dundrum. This was done, and my assessment, dated 17 October 1990, was sent off, but nothing came of it. I remember my brother saying that they were taking good care of Brendan's hand, which had been badly damaged by the suicide attempt in Spike Island. I said that repairing his hand without mental-health care would only enable him to handle a gun better.

When I did my assessment, I did not know that Doctors Charles Smith and Gerry O'Neill had already done a number of assessments over a period of two years.

Dr Smith gave evidence during the trial that Brendan was a very immature boy who was highly vulnerable to his older and more seriously delinquent companions. He said that it might not have been possible for the staff at Trinity House to have helped Brendan sufficiently because of the nature of his problems and the damage already done. However, he had hoped that, on his release, Brendan might have been persuaded to go to a residential family-type centre. In the event, Brendan did not serve his full sentence and they did not have enough time to persuade him to do this.

9

Return to Mountshannon

Tony Muggivan

B rendan was released from Dundrum in the spring of
1991 — I think it was March. He was now seventeen
years of age.

Whenever he was released, I kept a loaded shot gun in
bed with me at night. My wife was afraid I would shoot
her but she never insisted I put the gun away.

One day, he came and told me he wanted to park a
caravan. He said a friend of his, Fr Neylon, had bought a
caravan for him. I showed him where he could park it.

Within a very short time, two strange young men
visited him. I drove past on the tractor and saw Brendan
and the men. Brendan had a slash hook in his hands. I
thought he was cutting wood for the fire. He later told me
that the men had followed him from prison and had come
to beat him up but he had held them off with the slash
hook.

He asked me to call the health board to see if he could
get a better caravan when it began to leak. I phoned and

was referred to the Clare County Council. An inspector came to visit and look over the caravan. She seemed to think I could do more for him. She also said that there were people in worse conditions.

I believe that, at this time, Brendan was getting money from the health board every week. He had to go five miles to Scariff to pick it up.

I watched him as closely as I could throughout the year 1991. He did make an effort to improve. He bought a solid-wood stove for the caravan, as it was very cold. I told him he could cut all the firewood he wanted. He paid twenty-five pounds for the stove, which showed that he was able to save money.

He was getting his food from Sonny and Ann Farrell. One day, Sonny asked him to cut some firewood for him. Brendan refused and Sonny called him a lazy bastard. Brendan then told Sonny that he would 'get' him, and that ended their friendship.

Brendan used to dress up on Friday evenings and leave the village, heading in the direction of Scariff, and I wouldn't see him again till the following Monday or Tuesday. My son, Brendan, and his friend, Mick Starr, were in the hotel in Mountshannon and Mick's leather jacket was stolen. They told me about it on the following Sunday. I told them not to confront Brendan — that it was easy to push in the door of the caravan when he was not there. They did, and got the jacket back. Brendan never said anything about the jacket or what happened to it.

He continued to be very neat and clean in the way he dressed. However, the area around his caravan began to get filthy. He would throw out milk bottles and old papers and would never pick them up. One day, he asked me could he move the caravan into the trees where it would be hidden from view. He was afraid to be too near the road.

He called my brother, Tom Muggivan, and asked him about the use of his house. Tom owns a house near where he had his caravan. Tom told him that he would not be able to let him have the use of the house.

Brendan argued that he would be available to keep the house from being broken into, or even burned. Tom worried that Brendan was issuing a veiled threat that the house might be harmed if his request was rejected. However, Tom insisted, with pressure from his family, that he would not allow anyone to use the house.

Brendan later moved to a camping ground but was unhappy there. Three fishing rods were reported missing. He later moved into Fahys' house in Whitegate and I didn't see much of him after that. As discussed earlier, he told me that a guard had told him that I had set him up to be arrested by having him stay at my house and arranging for the guards to come and arrest him.

There were some hopeful signs that Brendan might settle down but it appeared unlikely that he would be able to get or hold stable employment.

JJ collected additional information on this phase of Brendan's life. What follows is what he wrote:

Denis Woods tried on several occasions to persuade him to settle down and he helped him as much as he could. He was driven part of the way to Ennis on one occasion by a friend of Denis Woods after he had agreed to enroll in a trade school. He was dropped off in Tulla having told the driver that he would hitch-hike the rest of the way.

The driver drove back toward Mountshannon but stopped on the way in Scariff to get groceries. When she arrived in Scariff, one of the first persons she saw on the street was Brendan. He had, apparently, hitched a ride

back to Scariff, instead of going on to Ennis, immediately after being dropped off in Tulla.

On another occasion, Denis tried to get him engaged
in some work on his farm, driving fence posts around
an area where he had collected his hay for the cattle for
the winter. The work required that stakes be driven into
the ground for the wire which would be strung around
the area to keep cattle out. Denis Woods was aware that
Brendan O'Donnell was a reluctant worker but he
nevertheless tried to get him to work.

Shortly after starting the work, Denis heard the
handle of the axe being used by Brendan cracking.
Brendan immediately reported that he could not now
work since he had no instrument to work with. He
appeared very disappointed when Denis Woods made
another handle for the axe and told Brendan that he
could now continue working.

From 1991 to 1992, Brendan continued to move from place
to place. It was reported that he committed a number of
break-ins during this time. He was charged with some of
them.

He was usually able to find people to help him. He was
given food, allowed to take showers, and allowed to do
his laundry. During this time, he had little trouble hitching
lifts on the roads. He travelled back and forth between
friends' houses and, frequently, travelled back and forth
between his grandmother's home in Eyrecourt and
Whitegate and Mountshannon. He could be an interesting
conversationalist. He would regularly visit Dinans in
Derrycon and be given meals. He sometimes spent hours
in conversation.

Brendan stole a boat cover to put over his caravan to
stop the leaking. I asked the owner of the boat cover and

the guards not to follow him up for stealing the cover as I feared he would come after the owner at a later date.

An elderly man, Willie Keane, was beaten up one night while returning home from the village. He was badly beaten and had to be hospitalised for a number of days. I later found out that Willie Keane had ordered Brendan out of his hay shed. Brendan had been sleeping in the shed at night.

Around this time, he robbed the late Mr Smythe and stole his car. I had a conversation with Mr Smythe and he told me that he could have shot Brendan but he felt sorry for him and gave him about eighty pounds. Brendan took his car and it was later found in a lake in County Galway.

10

Assault on Ann Marie

JJ Muggivan

A fter leaving Mountshannon, Brendan went to live in Whitegate with a man named Denis Fahy, and his son, Derek. Shortly afterwards, Denis Fahy drowned.

Denis Fahy went swimming late in the evening or night of 2 September 1992, having been in the village of Whitegate with his friends. It seems that some friends challenged him to jump in the harbour at Williamstown Quay. The water was about nine feet deep.

Brendan and Derek Fahy were present.

After he had jumped in the water, it became immediately apparent that Denis Fahy was in difficulty. His son jumped to help him while Brendan O'Donnell ran for help. Efforts to save the man failed and his body was recovered next day by Denis Tirnan and some locals.

Brendan was a good swimmer and seemed to have felt some guilt at not having done more to save his friend. He later commented a number of times that he regretted not trying to do more.

A number of news reports suggested that Brendan had problems with drinking. These reports are not true. He rarely had more than a couple of drinks on any occasion. When he drank, he would sing and, according to his sister, he wasn't a bad singer. During one of her visits to Dundrum, she heard him give a fairly good rendition of 'The Fields of Athenry'.

When Denis Fahy drowned, Brendan moved in with Denis Woods in Mountshannon. After staying there for a while, he moved to Ballinasloe and into an apartment near his sister, Ann Marie.

He next left for England, going to Wolverhampton. Not long after arriving there, he was arrested for snatching a woman's handbag. He was imprisoned for a while and when he was released, he returned to Whitegate.

What follows is Ann Marie's account of his return:

An argument broke out one night in the family home in Whitegate after Brendan had returned from England the previous night. His father had gone outside to lock the car. I knew I could hear people talking outside but I didn't know for a while it was Brendan. He came inside the house to the sitting room and I was surprised to see him. He was after telling us he had to leave England and come home to Ireland, as there were fellas after him and maybe even the police in England. He was after stealing an old lady's handbag.

After he had told us all of the story of what had happened, with a lot of persuasion of my father, I asked him to let Brendan stay that night as it was bitterly cold outside and where else had he to go.

In the end, he let him stay but told him that in the morning he would have to go. I made up a bed for him in my room and prepared something for him to eat, as he was hungry.

The next morning, he asked him was he ready to leave the house and my father told him he would bring him some distance in the car. He made it quite clear to him he didn't want him in the house and it would be best for everyone if he left. He drove him a few miles from Whitegate and when he [Brendan] got out of the car he hitched a lift to my grandparents in Eyrecourt. He went to see his grandmother and later he went to see Fr Neylon.

I rang my grandmother later that night to see did he arrive there and she said he did.

She also said that herself and other family relatives would drop Brendan back up to Whitegate that night as there was little they could do to help him and he was very much his father's responsibility and it was up to him to take care of him as he was his father.

They eventually did arrive in Whitegate with him and my father was angry with them for bringing him up after he told him that morning to go.

Then an argument took place and he told Brendan to leave the house once again, as he was showing him the way to the front door, and he threw him out of the house. Brendan's words were, 'Fine, I'll go. I know you don't care about me anyway', and he gave his father a good kick in the shins.

Before he left that night, I gave him some money and asked him to let me know where he would be eventually when he got settled somewhere, as he left his home that night with nowhere to go and I did not know what was going to happen next. He told me he would keep in touch with me. I said goodbye to him and he left once again with his relatives, to go where nobody knew or seemed to care. I did, but I just couldn't do anything to help him or I didn't know exactly what I could do, nor neither did my grandmother know what to do. As far as I can remember back I think he went back, again to Fr Neylon.

After the problems with his father, Brendan was able to get some more help from Fr Neylon and he moved into a flat in Portumna. He was soon followed to Portumna by Ann Marie, who began living in a flat in the same building close to him. This was in the autumn of 1992. He was now eighteen-and-a-half years old.

After moving into the flat in Portumna in the autumn of 1992, Brendan dated a girl for a while, but she eventually broke off the relationship.

Ann Marie reports that her brother was now clearly, and obviously, not well. She gave me a detailed description of Brendan's assault on her and her baby, with a knife. She later described this attack for the court during his trial.

It is revealing to contrast that event with her account of what happened between them a few months earlier on his return from England, and which shows her affection for her brother. She had already chosen him to be her baby's godfather.

Did Brendan become fully delusional after the drowning of Denis Fahy and the rejection by his father on his return from England? Was it after the events of late 1992 that Brendan truly crossed the threshold from Post-Traumatic Stress Disorder to a psychotic disorder?

The attack on Ann Marie has new, and ominous, features.

Ann Marie was staying in a flat with her seven-month-old child, and Brendan had a room nearby. One day, Brendan came to his sister's apartment and asked her to make him a sandwich.

She said that she was feeding her baby and that she would prepare the sandwich as soon as she finished. He said that if she didn't make the sandwich immediately, he would get a knife and stab her. With these words, he suddenly snatched a knife off the table and swung it directly at her face. She managed to get her hands up in front of her, grabbing his hand with both of hers. She forced his hand downwards causing the knife to penetrate her leg just below her knee.

She later showed me the knife, which is still part of her kitchen cutlery. It was about six inches long, had a black handle, and a stainless-steel blade. It looked like a steak knife except that the blade was not serrated. It was sharp and was pointed.

Ann Marie escaped into the bedroom with her baby but was unable to get the door locked behind her to prevent her brother from following her. When he entered the bedroom, he kept her cornered and away from the door. He sat on the window ledge and pulled out a switchblade. He began flicking the blade in and out of its handle.

Brendan ordered Ann Marie not to move. She had placed the baby on the bed and was standing some distance away. He stabbed the switch-blade into the mattress beside the baby's head several times, cutting the duvet. The blade hit very close to the baby's head.

Throughout the following hours of captivity, Ann Marie made numerous attempts to manipulate an escape with her baby. Brendan responded to all of her efforts by saying that she was only trying to outsmart him in order to escape.

The incident lasted up to three or four hours. The baby got hungry and began to cry. Ann Marie noticed that Brendan was beginning to appear frightened about how it might end up for him. He seemed to have become aware that he was now in a predicament that he was going to have trouble getting out of.

She suddenly said that she could hear footsteps outside the door. Brendan walked out of the bedroom. As soon as he was outside, Ann Marie managed to get the door locked. She began to shout for a man who lived downstairs. After a while, she was able to get his attention. She tried to warn him to be very careful about coming up the stairs, that her brother had a knife, and that he could be very dangerous.

She recalled that the man, very coolly, walked up the stairs, whistling. When Ann Marie opened the door, her neighbour very casually asked her what was going on. At this point, she decided that she could safely leave the room with the baby.

She went downstairs with the man and began making plans to call somebody to get help. Suddenly, Brendan, who she thought had left the apartment, came out with an axe. She later discovered that he had both a hatchet and an axe in his room, and that he had had them for some time.

Ann Marie went to the garda station. She was told that the guards were out somewhere and that there was no one at the station except the sergeant. She was in a state of panic at what she thought unfairly was a lack of urgency on the part of the sergeant. She told him that Brendan was crazy and could be roaming around, and that he had watched her coming down the street. He had been walking on the other side of the street and he had tried to persuade her not to do anything. She tried to communicate as best she could that Brendan was dangerous and that something needed to be done quickly.

The sergeant made arrangements for her to go to a local doctor, Dr Fionnuala Kennedy, because of the stab wound below her knee. She went to the doctor. Upon hearing her account of what happened, Dr Kennedy made arrangements to have Brendan committed to Ballinasloe Hospital.

This incident happened in 1992 at the end of September or the beginning of October. It was within weeks, or at the most a couple of months, of the drowning of Denis Fahy. It was about one year and eight months before the killings.

Brendan was picked up and taken to St Bridget's Hospital in Ballinasloe. On his arrival at the hospital, there was confusion as to who should sign the committal orders. Ann Marie agreed that if they asked his father to sign the committal orders, he might refuse, and if Brendan ever discovered that his father had signed the committal orders, he might eventually harm his father.

Ann Marie signed the committal papers but did not tell her brother that she had done so. He believed that the guards had signed the papers and he was not told otherwise.

According to Ann Marie, Brendan 'had a very powerful animosity toward guards'. He always referred to them as the 'dirt-bags'. When he was screaming at her from the other side of the street, when she was on her way to the garda station, he had kept shouting, 'Don't go to the dirt-bags!'

Ann Marie was shocked a couple of weeks later to find that her brother had been released from the hospital and was back in the neighbourhood. She was more shocked when she heard a report — attributed to a nurse from Ballinasloe who was visiting people in the community — that Brendan had convinced the hospital staff that he was mentally stable but that she was the one with problems.

He had reportedly elaborated on his belief that his sister had been trying to poison him and, apparently, had told a convincing story about her being insane. It was reported during Brendan's trial that he told staff at Ballinasloe that his sister put poison in milk he was about to drink. Ann Marie worried for some time that people from Ballinasloe Hospital might come to pick her up and have her committed.

While in Ballinasloe Psychiatric Hospital, Brendan was diagnosed as having paranoid ideation. This was his second trip to Ballinasloe, the first having been with Tony about three-and-a-half years earlier. The hospital appears to have done a very limited assessment and did not interview his sister. Ann Marie believes that Dr Kennedy was not interviewed either.

Dr Kennedy gave evidence at the trial that she had asked gardaí to take Brendan to the psychiatric hospital. She regarded him as a danger to Ann Marie, her child, himself and anyone he might meet. She had first encountered him in late September 1992 when he had come to her surgery. He was eighteen at the time and had given her a brief life history.

Dr Kennedy recalled that Brendan had phoned her late on the night of 12 November 1992, and had asked her to come to his sister's flat. He told the doctor that Ann Marie had fallen off a chair while putting up curtains. When the doctor called to the flat, Brendan met her outside and followed her in. He closed the door behind them and stood at it with his arms folded. She felt wary about him and thought that he had a strange attitude.

The doctor said that she found bruising on Ann Marie's side and that Ann Marie repeated Brendan's story about having fallen while putting up curtains.

When Brendan attacked his sister with the knife, Dr Kennedy treated her for a puncture wound to her knee. Ann Marie admitted on that occasion that she had not fallen off the chair on 12 November, but had been attacked by her brother. Brendan had accused her of making duplicate keys to his flat and had punched her. He had given the same reason for stabbing her.

Prior to giving her testimony at Brendan's trial, Ann Marie realised that Brendan had never found out who had signed the committal orders for Ballinasloe Hospital. She realised that he was going to hear who it was for the first time when she testified. She checked to make sure that she was safe in the courtroom before giving this particular piece of testimony.

When she finished with this testimony, Ann Marie decided to look at her brother to see what impact it had had on him. She was surprised to see an amused expression on his face, as if to acknowledge that she had outsmarted him.

11

Worsening Mental Health

JJ Muggivan

Brendan's assault on Ann Marie and her baby is the most significant milestone on his journey. It represents a dramatic turning point in his life. He had shown signs for some time of being extremely paranoid, but now there could be little doubt about what had become his primary mental-health disorder.

He had Delusional Disorder, Paranoid Type. Having paranoid ideation, as diagnosed by Ballinasloe Hospital, is much less severe and might not have made him as dangerous. He was now clearly dangerous and, if the circumstances were right, he could kill.

Clearly the diagnosis made by Dr Smith and Dr O'Neill in 1988–90 was correct. They referred to delusions and psychosis without being specific as to what type.

Brendan left Ballinasloe Hospital a dangerous man for two reasons. Firstly, he had a mental-health disorder that had brought him to the point of killing his sister and her baby. Secondly, he left the hospital with additional reasons to run from the authorities. He had just committed another crime — the assault on Ann Marie and her baby.

The assault on his sister and baby, and the decision of Ballinasloe Hospital to release him, are the starting points of the journey which led directly to the deaths of Imelda Riney, her child, and Fr Walsh — and ultimately, to Brendan's own death.

Ironically, Ballinasloe Hospital came very close to a correct diagnosis. 'Paranoid ideation' is similar to Paranoid Delusional Disorder, but is less serious and does not make the individual as dangerous. Paranoid ideation is defined as follows:

> [I]deation, of less than delusional proportions, involving suspiciousness or the belief that one is being harassed, persecuted, or unfairly treated. (DSM-IV-TR, p. 826)

Brendan's story so far shows that he clearly suffered from paranoia for most of his life. He had particular paranoia about being poisoned by germs in food. He may have had this fear as early as one of his first visits to a doctor when he was four or five years of age, when he said that he was seeing animals in his food.

His appetite became so poor at that stage that he was given medication to help him to eat. He remained obsessed with germs: he wouldn't eat in certain houses; he would check dishes and cups before using them, and would clean them himself.

He was so paranoid about germs on dishes and in food that he annoyed Tony's sons with his finickiness. The incident of Brendan Muggivan wiping the floor with a slice of bread and eating it to demonstrate that it wouldn't poison him was a challenge, not to 'paranoid ideation' but to a 'paranoid belief'.

The assault on Ann Marie having demonstrated that Brendan at this point had full-blown Paranoid Delusional Disorder, this is a good time to describe and explain what that is.

'Paranoid ideation', as diagnosed in Ballinasloe Psychiatric Hospital, can cause an individual to act against people whom they believe are perpetrating harassment, persecution, or unfair treatment against them. But they usually do not act with the same intensity or consistency as an individual with Delusional Disorder, Persecutory Type. They will rarely attempt to kill someone based on an erroneous ideation. A paranoid delusion is different. It makes the individual much more dangerous.

A delusion, as opposed to ideation, is a false belief someone has formed, based on an incorrect assessment of a situation. The person with the belief holds to it strongly, in spite of what almost everyone else believes and in spite of any absolute proof that might show that the belief is false. When such a belief involves a very extreme and incredible value judgement, it is regarded as delusional.

A persecutory or paranoid delusion is when:

> ... the central theme of the delusion involves the person's belief that he or she is being conspired against, cheated, spied on, followed, *poisoned* [emphasis added], or drugged, maliciously maligned, harassed, or obstructed in the pursuit of long-term goals. (DSM-IV-TR, p. 325)

In the case of a paranoid delusion, a person will exaggerate small slights, seeing them as injustices that should be remedied.

> Individuals with persecutory delusions are often resentful and angry and may resort to violence against those they believe are hurting them. (Ibid., p. 325)

102

All of the above describes Brendan O'Donnell. Throughout his life, one of the beliefs that frightened Brendan was that he was being poisoned. This fear eventually made him dangerous, bringing him to the stage where he could have killed his sister. His sister warded off one attack and demonstrated that it wouldn't be easy to kill her with a knife. When Brendan got his hands on an axe, she had already escaped from her bedroom.

It was one of his delusional beliefs that kept Brendan's 'fight' and 'flight' response to danger constantly active. His avoidance of food was his 'flight' response. He was ready to kill as his 'fight' response became more active.

Can stressful events or stressful circumstances make the symptoms of Paranoid Delusional Disorder worse? Can stressful events or circumstances push an individual with 'paranoid ideation' over the edge to Paranoid Delusional Disorder?

I believe the answer is yes. In the months before the assault on Ann Marie, Brendan had several stressful experiences. He had witnessed his friend's drowning. He had been arrested in England and was running from the law.

He was rejected by his father and put out of his home after returning from England. He saw his family in confusion about where he could or should live. The night he was put out of his father's home, Brendan kicked his father on the shins in anger at the rejection.

All of the foregoing happened to a young man who already had chronic mental-health disorders. Even if he did not have Post-Traumatic Stress Disorder for most of his life, he was exposed to a belief system most of his life which saw the world as dangerous.

Because of all the hurt he suffered, whether by accident or human design, it is not surprising that he could have developed a dominant belief that he was being 'conspired against, cheated, spied on, followed, *poisoned*, or drugged, maliciously maligned, harassed, or obstructed in the pursuit of long-term goals'.

Brendan had only one goal in life and that was to survive the dangers he felt were all around him. Sometimes the dangers he felt were real, such as the danger of being raped or beaten in state institutions; such as not getting mental-health treatment; such as his mother dying by her own hands, and so on.

In attempting to run from dangers, imagined and real, he would usually create additional real problems for himself. He would run from court dates, steal cars to get away, break into houses, destroy the cars he stole to hide signs of his involvement, and so on.

Understanding his state of mind makes it possible to understand his behaviour. Understanding his beliefs and fears and their connection to his behaviour is as simple as understanding that his fear of green men in his bedroom caused him to want to sleep with his mother or sister for safety and protection.

Until now I have explained Brendan's 'fight' or 'flight' behaviour. However, there was another feature of his delusional disorder that does not explain adequately all of his violent behaviour. He sometimes assaulted people when he was not trying to 'flee' danger or 'fight' people whom he felt were dangerous to him.

The assault on Willie Keane and the assault on the workman in Whitegate are examples. When Brendan found out that Tony had helped the guards in their failed attempt to arrest him, he later threatened Tony on the phone that he would 'get' someone close to him. People were scared of him because they believed he would take revenge if they didn't try to appease him. People were scared not to pick him up whenever he was on the road hitch-hiking.

Brendan O'Donnell

NAME Brendan. O. Donnell. .... NUMBER. 416.....

PLACE OF DETENTION,
WHEATFIELD,
CLONDALKIN,
DUBLIN 22.

...... 4. -11 .... 19 90 ....

Hi tony just a few lines hopeing you are
Well And family tell Mary Vera And Everybody
That I was asking for them I write a
letter to JJ a couple of weeks ago
how are things going for you on the
farm tell Josephine I was asking for her
I write her a letter but she Never Replied back
Well tony as for Myself i am alright And My
hand has Improved great well tony tell Dermot and
Micheal that I was asking for them When you
See them. I hope you have the flag flying
Anyway tony if you see David around tell him
I was asking for him. how is Kevin getting On
In Flannans colleuage try to come up to see
Me Soon well Tony thats all I have to say
for Now So Until I hear from you again
So goodbye Takecare
                    Brendan.
ps write back soon

AH1519

A letter from Brendan to Tony

Imelda Riney

Liam Riney

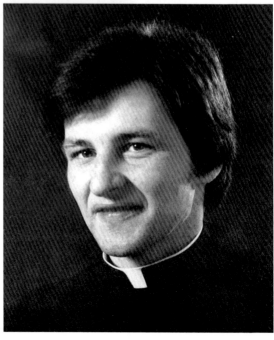

Fr Joe Walsh

Imelda Riney's house in Whitegate

Fr Walsh's car at Williamstown Pier, Whitegate

Fiona Sampson

Edward Cleary

The funeral of Imelda and Liam Riney

A grotto dedicated to Imelda and Liam in the forest where they were killed

A cross marks the spot where Fr Joe Walsh was shot

The Muggivan family: Tony, Brendan, Kevin, Gerard,
Ross and Mary

JJ Muggivan

In other words, he was dangerously vindictive and capable of seeking revenge against those he believed had harmed him or would harm him. The guidelines for identifying persecutory delusions describe Brendan so well they could have been written for him:

> *Individuals with persecutory delusions are often resentful and angry and may resort to violence against those they believe are hurting them* [emphasis added]. (DSM-IV-TR, p. 325)

Should an individual with full-blown, untreated Paranoid Delusional Disorder, severe and chronic, be determined to be fit to stand trial for his actions as one who is legally sane? It is a difficult disorder on which to make a determination because many with the disorder can appear sane much, or even most, of the time. DSM-IV-TR addresses this point:

> [With Delusional Disorder] Psychosocial functioning is variable. Some individuals may appear to be relatively unimpaired in their interpersonal and occupational roles. In others, the impairment may be substantial and include low or absent occupational functioning. When poor psychosocial functioning is present in Delusional Disorder, it arises directly from the delusional beliefs themselves. (DSM-IV-TR, p. 324)

This point will be addressed again since by the time of his trial Brendan had more serious problems than Delusional Disorder — or any of the other disorders he had had throughout his life.

Shortly after his release from Ballinasloe Hospital and before his trial date in Portumna, scheduled for sometime at the end of 1993, for the several incidents which had taken place throughout 1992, Brendan O'Donnell left for England again.

Margaret Maher, Fr Joseph Walsh's sister, reported that Brendan broke into the curate's house in Eyrecourt in about March of 1993 and stole one of her brother's suits. It was reported that he left for England dressed as a priest.

Not long after arriving in England, Brendan was arrested for the handbag theft he had committed when he was there previously. He was tried for the incident, and sentenced to one year in prison.

He spent the next year, March 1993 to March 1994, either in prison or in hospital in England, apparently in Wolverhampton or somewhere nearby. Medical reports from the prison 'showed concern about Mr O'Donnell's mental state' (*The Irish Times*, 15 March 1996, Testimony of Dr Turrall, Psychologist).

In the late summer of 1993, Tony met Imelda Riney on the road outside Son O'Donnell's house in Whitegate, and near where she lived. She pulled up in her car and started a conversation. She had two children with her in the car. She asked Tony for slates to fix the roof of the house where she was living.

She had bought the house but it needed a lot of repairs. Its owner, Willie Gleeson, had recently died. Tony knew that Brendan had stayed in this house off and on for a number of years and before his move to the apartment in Portumna.

The slates were in Son O'Donnell's yard. Son O'Donnell was Brendan's grand-uncle. Imelda Riney had previously asked Son O'Donnell about the slates and he had referred her to Tony. Tony now told her that she could have whatever number of slates she needed.

During the conversation, she began talking to Tony about Brendan, commenting on what a nice boy he was.

From the manner in which she was talking, and the details she seemed to know about his life, it was clear to Tony that she must have had fairly extensive conversations with him and about him. She probably would also have heard much about him from Son O'Donnell.

She mentioned to Tony that Brendan had told her that Tony was the only one willing to help him with all of his difficulties. Tony felt she spoke caringly of him. He did not answer her in any great detail as he did not, at this time, have the same opinions of Brendan as she seemed to believe he had.

He recalled a conversation he had had with Brendan the previous year, 1992, during which Brendan had talked about meeting a particular woman, with two small children, at the Health Centre in Scariff. He recalled Brendan telling him that the woman with the children had admired the sweater Mary had bought for him after he first came to his home.

From things Imelda Riney said about Brendan, Tony realised that she was the woman Brendan had talked to him about. At the time, he had wondered if Brendan had developed an interest in this woman. He even wondered if he had a fantasy about asking her to marry him and if this was his reason for asking for a plot of ground. He had told Brendan that she was not for him and he had never heard Brendan speak of her again.

Imelda Riney was well liked by the locals and was seen as a caring mother to her children. She regularly stopped in to see Brendan's grand-uncle on her way to Whitegate village for groceries, and she would ask him if he wanted anything from the shop.

When she was later reported missing, Son O'Donnell took her loss very hard and, indeed, her death and the deaths of the other victims, may have hastened his own. He died very shortly after the killings. Many of his relatives and many locals believe that he was another victim of the tragic events.

For Imelda Riney to show signs that she might care enough to befriend Brendan could be dangerous as far as Tony was concerned. He recalls worrying about the possibility of there being a friendship between them. However, as far as he knew, at the time of this conversation, Brendan was in jail in England, so he gave no more thought to his worries until after the events of April/May 1994.

12

Return from England

JJ Muggivan

Brendan returned from England shortly after being released from jail on 25 March 1994. He came into Ireland through Belfast and hitched rides from Belfast to the Eyrecourt area.

He was not supposed to leave England as he was on probation until the end of his sentence. He came through Belfast to avoid any greater scrutiny there might have been had he returned home through another entry point, such as Dublin or Cork in the Republic of Ireland.

He went to his grandmother's in Eyrecourt after arriving. Members of the Quinn family did not want him living with Mary Quinn as they believed him to be dangerous. Because of this, he had to hide from the relatives when he stayed with his grandmother. If there was danger of his being seen by a relative, he would leave and stay wherever he could until it was safe to return.

While in Eyrecourt, he told his uncle, Michael Quinn (his mother's brother), about his problems with the law and how he was in danger of being arrested if he wasn't careful. Michael Quinn didn't want Brendan staying with his parents (Brendan's grandparents) and made this known to him. He told Brendan to give himself up to the guards and to stop running from them. Brendan told him that he would think about it. However, he seemed to get suspicious that his uncle would turn him in to the guards. He felt it was no longer safe for him to be in Eyrecourt and he asked his uncle to drive him to Mountshannon.

Brendan was seen by several people shortly after arriving in the Mountshannon and Whitegate area. He set up a 'home' in Cregg Forest, near his original home in Cregg Wood. It is likely that he used plastic covering or bales of hay as covering at night. Years earlier, Tony had asked him how he kept warm at night when he slept outdoors. He told him that a good way to keep warm was to wrap onself up in plastic since it was air- and water-proof and would keep in the heat and keep out the damp. Tony wrote of where Brendan was staying:

> I believe his 'home' was about a quarter of a mile into Cregg Forest from Cregg Cross. After the tragedy of the following weeks, I noticed a mirror placed in a tree where the lights from a car entering the same area would flash. By checking the angle of the mirror, I believe I located the exact place where he was staying. It was at this location I later found a sock which I believe I had seen Imelda Riney wearing.

Shortly after arriving, Brendan made contact with Ms Mae Tuohy, the local postwoman. Mae Tuohy was well acquainted with the O'Donnell family and had befriended Brendan many times when he was growing up. She was again willing to help him since she knew he had no job and probably had no money.

Mae Tuohy brought Brendan groceries on a number of occasions, meeting him near what is known as 'The Mill'. 'The Mill' is located about one mile from his original family home and close to the part of Cregg Forest where Brendan now had his 'home'. Mae Tuohy would usually bring him the groceries at around four o'clock in the afternoon. Tony recalled seeing Brendan around this time:

Not long after Brendan arrived back from England, in about the middle of April 1994, I was having a conversation with a friend of his, Paddy Bugler, when Brendan passed us in a fairly new car. Paddy Bugler commented that he would be willing to bet that the car was not a car he had purchased.

I was surprised to discover that Brendan was again in the area and was even more surprised that he had not come to visit me. I was aware that Brendan would not stop to talk to me while he was in the car he was driving because he would feel that he would have to explain to me where he had got it.

My wife and I were preparing to make a trip to Cologne in Germany, to visit some friends. I called JJ in New Orleans and we discussed our fears about Brendan being back in the area and the likelihood that he had already stolen a car.

JJ warned me to make sure that all of my guns were safely hidden before we left for Germany. I told him that I had already hidden the guns and that I had hidden the ammunition in a different location. We agreed that all members of the family should be warned not to be alone with him, not to pick him up on the road if they were alone in the car, and to be alert for danger signs should they come in contact with him.

I owned a three-shot, semi-automatic shotgun. Brendan was familiar with this gun, and this caused me to be more aware of the need for caution.

During this month, it was reported that Brendan was driving a car on the Shannon road in Mountshannon when he saw his father working with some other council men. He reportedly attempted to run over his father with the car, but his father managed to jump out of the way before being hit. I heard a report that Brendan was seen laughing as he drove away.

While in Germany, I called my brother numerous times to discuss my worries. We both agreed that it would be useless to contact the guards until some crime had been committed.

Some time later, and about two or three weeks after his arrival in the area, Brendan stopped showing up for his meetings with Mae Tuohy. He had apparently found another source of food.

A few weeks after setting up tent in Cregg Forest, Brendan seems to have gone looking for an empty house instead. On Thursday evening, 20 April, he went by his grand-uncle's house near the old house where he had previously stayed. The old house was that previously owned by Willie Gleeson from Limerick. It had been used by Willie Gleeson as a holiday home, so most of the time it was empty.

While talking to his grand-uncle, Brendan noticed smoke coming out of the chimney of the old house and he asked his uncle who was living there now. Son O'Donnell told him that Imelda Riney lived there with her two children. He told him not to bother the woman and her children and to find somewhere else to live. Brendan, however, made contact with Imelda Riney, and seems to have asked her for help.

13

Looking for Help

JJ Muggivan

The following is a reconstruction of Brendan's movements, based on trial testimony, published reports and interviews.

It may have been under Imelda Riney's persuasion that Brendan decided to make contact with the Muggivans. He walked from Cregg Wood to Muggivans' not long after making contact with Imelda Riney.

He found Brendan Muggivan and Vera O'Sullivan, Brendan Muggivan's maternal aunt, at the house. Brendan Muggivan and Vera were busy with the evening chores and were very cool to him. They gave him little encouragement to stay. They were both watchful and nervous, and they noticed that Brendan was too. He asked them where Tony and Mary were and they told him that they were in Germany.

Brendan Muggivan asked him where he was staying, and he said he was staying over in Cregg in a tent.

He asked for food and Brendan prepared some hot dogs for him. Brendan O'Donnell sarcastically asked if that was the best he could do. Brendan Muggivan told him that that was all he was going to get. Later, he asked to be driven back to Cregg Forest.

Brendan Muggivan was nervous at having Brendan around and, because he could not leave him alone, was glad to hear he wanted to leave. He reluctantly agreed to drive him, remembering his father's warning never to be alone with him in a car. He decided the risk was worth it, however, in order to have him leave. He knew that he could not leave him alone in the house while he completed his chores.

Brendan Muggivan believed he was taking a serious risk by driving Brendan O'Donnell to Cregg Wood but he did not like the alternatives of having him stay longer at the house or become angry. Both young men were quiet during the four-mile trip to Cregg Wood.

It is not known if, at this time, Brendan was in possession of the single shot .22 rifle and the large quantity of ammunition that he stole from Ned Jameson in Whitegate.

Brendan Muggivan drove to Cregg Cross but Brendan O'Donnell wanted to be driven into the wood. Brendan Muggivan refused to go further and told Brendan that he would have to walk the rest of the way. He gave the excuse that he was in a hurry home to finish the evening chores. He said goodnight and drove home.

On Thursday evening, 28 April, the evening preceding the abduction of Imelda Riney and her child, Brendan got a lift from Limerick with Maudie Nash. He told her that his 'fucking head was not too good', and she was nervous of him. On his return to Mountshannon, he again came to the Muggivans'. This time, he was met by Brendan

Muggivan, Vera O'Sullivan, and her future husband, Joe O'Rourke.

He again asked when Tony and Mary would be returning from Germany. They told him that they would not be back for at least another week.

All three made sure to have Brendan under constant observation as he was acting very suspiciously. They continued to believe he wanted to get his hands on the automatic shotgun.

After staying for a while, he again asked to be driven to Cregg Forest. This time, Brendan Muggivan refused to drive him, remembering the fear he had felt on the previous occasion.

After the events of the weekend, locals reported that, at this time, Brendan had already stolen the single shot .22 rifle and a large quantity of ammunition. Mrs Brady said that she met him on Thursday evening and that he had a rifle or a shotgun inside his overcoat.

It was still Thursday night, 28 April 1994. Brendan left Muggivans' very angry. He walked down the road from Derrycon towards Mountshannon village.

About a quarter of a mile down the road, he stopped at Frank Muggivan's. Frank Muggivan, another brother of mine, lived in a mobile home near the side of the road.

Frank put on the kettle to make some tea and, to make conversation, asked Brendan what he had been doing since he had seen him last, and when he had come back to the area. Brendan talked little but was agitated and disorganised. He appeared frightened and worried.

During the conversation, he stated that he was planning on going abroad shortly — that he was not going to be spending much time in the area. Around Mountshannon, the expression 'going abroad' usually means going some place other than England. The expression is most often used when someone is planning on going to the Continent.

Frank did not see any sign of a gun on Brendan. As both men were talking, waiting for the kettle to boil, they heard a car driving up the road from the direction of Mountshannon. They saw the headlights through the window. Suddenly, the car turned into the yard. It was moving fast and, when it came into the yard, it hit a bicycle standing against a fence. Frank went outside to see what the commotion was.

It was a squad car with two guards. Both guards got out of the car and Frank greeted them. He had just spoken to the guards when Brendan leapt out the door behind him, shouting at the guards to back off. He had his right hand in his coat pocket as if holding a handgun.

The suddenness of Brendan's appearance, his shout, his demeanour, and the signs that he had a gun, startled Frank and caused the guards to jump backwards. Brendan immediately ran across the road and into a field.

The guards did not pursue. They were unarmed.

When the guards left, Frank turned off the kettle and started walking up the road to Tony's house. This was the last known contact anyone had with Brendan before the abduction of Imelda Riney and her child the following morning.

There are no live witnesses who can report conversations with Brendan from about ten o'clock on Thursday night, 28 April, to about 3.30 p.m. on Saturday afternoon, 30 April. We have only sketchy accounts of his movements, and knowledge about where he had to have been, based on the trail of evidence he left.

We have his testimony — the testimony he gave immediately after he was captured is probably the most reliable. The testimony he gave at the trial is not as reliable for two

116

reasons. Firstly, he wanted to convince the jury that he was insane, so he had to embellish his motivation for his actions. Secondly, by the time of the trial, he probably had new brain injuries from his medicine, and it is very likely that his memory and intellectual functioning were even more severely impaired.

This makes it necessary to construct some stages of this account from known facts, his testimony, and the events that happened. This construction starts with Brendan leaving Derrycon on Thursday night and continues until he arrives in Eyrecourt on Saturday afternoon. I believe the following is reliable and substantially accurate.

Brendan began his walk back to Cregg Wood. The guards drove down to the village of Mountshannon at pub-closing time.

The publican got angry at the guards and told them that they would be serving the people better if they were out trying to capture Brendan O'Donnell. He said that if they knew how to do their jobs, they would be up in Derrycon, checking to see if one of the Muggivans was hiding O'Donnell from the law.

The guards left the bar angry, and drove back to Derrycon. They overtook Frank on the road as he walked up to Tony's house. They again confronted him but this time they were belligerent.

Meanwhile, Brendan's mind was in turmoil. His fears were now intensified. He had just encountered two guards who he believed were already searching for him. He believed it was known that he had jumped probation in England.

He knew that the guards would still want him for having run away from his court date in Portumna for his assault on his sister and her baby. He also knew that they would want to question him about the theft of the car he had stolen a couple of weeks earlier.

He walked down the road towards Mountshannon as soon as he saw the guards leaving Frank Muggivan's. He was ready to jump into a field at the first appearance of a car — either the sound of a car or the lights. At the bridge, halfway to Mountshannon, he took a left turn and walked up Dinan's Road, planning to journey to Cregg Forest by the back roads.

His mind had been racing for weeks, worsening every day. He now had to have a plan. He had to have a plan that could be put into effect as soon as possible. He could not stay another day in the Mountshannon, Whitegate, or Eyrecourt areas. Indeed, it was now urgent that he not stay any longer in Ireland.

He concluded that the guards now believed he was armed and dangerous and that soon every guard and policemen in Ireland and England would be searching for him. He had to get to France.

Tony would not be back from Germany for another week, and he might not get help from him anyway. Imelda Riney was now his only hope. He went back to his tent and began making preparations for the next day.

Brendan said during his trial that he got a lift back to Cregg Forest that Thursday night, but no witness ever came forward to corroborate this.

14

The Killing of Imelda and Liam Riney — A Reconstruction

JJ Muggivan

Imelda Riney awoke early. She knew that Brendan would be coming to the house after Val Ballance, her ex-husband, picked up their older son, Oisín, to take him to school. She hoped that she would be finished with Brendan today.

She hoped that he had made contact with Tony and that Tony had helped him. She was scared to think of anything else. She was frightened by his talk of robbing the post office in Whitegate, and having her help him.

She did not know how he might act if she refused to help him, although she was sure that she could not, and would not, help him commit a robbery. He had told her a few days earlier that he would like to have Tony's automatic gun. She hoped against hope that he had not succeeded in stealing it.

She knew that Tony would not give him a gun but, instead, would think of a way to help him. Imelda decided that if Tony helped Brendan with money, she would be willing to drive him to Cork to help him begin his journey to France. She would even promise to follow him later if this would get rid of the more immediate danger.

Soon after she got up, Imelda Riney noticed that Val Ballance was already up. He had been around for the past few days and was helping her with the children. It was about 7.30 or 8.00. Val prepared breakfast and he and the two children ate. Imelda usually didn't eat breakfast. She helped get Oisín ready for school and, when everyone had finished breakfast, she said goodbye to Val and Oisín, Val brought Oisín to a neighbour who would give him a lift to school.

Imelda told Val that she would come over to the school in Tuamgraney later in the day and bring lunch with her. This was the last time Val and Oisín saw her and Liam alive.

She went back into the house with Liam and began nervously cleaning up after breakfast. She was talking to Liam. She had been anxious that he would begin talking about Brendan. He had begun to call him Ben although he had initially been nervous around him.

A few hours later — at about 10.30 — she heard sounds outside, followed by a knock on the door. She knew who it was but she had to answer. She had feared that Brendan might be waiting outside until he was sure that Val had left with Oisín.

She opened the door and saw Brendan standing there with a rifle.

He attempted to come inside with the gun. In her shock, she shouted at him to leave the gun outside, that she would not allow a gun in her house. He told her they had to go ahead with the post office robbery.

He left the gun outside and came in. She tried to argue with him.

He would not be persuaded and told her that they had very little time. The van bringing the money from Scariff Post Office to Whitegate Post Office had passed a couple of hours previously. The longer they waited, the less cash would be left in the post office. The garda escort had already returned to Scariff and there would be no guard around.

Imelda was panicking and desperately trying to stop Brendan from going ahead with his plans. He was speaking intensely and urgently. The money was delivered in cash and, not long after delivery, most of the cash would be picked up by the pensioners and others who received money.

She became just as insistent that she could not help him but tried to settle him down by offering to make him some tea and prepare a breakfast. She put water in the kettle and started the gas fire. Brendan began to become irate and shouted at her to get the child ready and to get in the car.

He retrieved the rifle and threatened her and the child if they would not do as ordered.

She tried to slow him down but he demanded sex. They went upstairs. Brendan would state at his trial that Imelda consented to sex. Her family, however, insists that she would never have consented.

Fear now consumed her, mostly for her child. Brendan had no intentions of giving up on his plans to rob the post office. Imelda tried not to show her fear in order to keep the child from becoming frightened. She put on Liam's blue wellingtons and his coat. She put on her own coat and took her son to the car. Brendan was walking behind her, hiding the rifle inside his jacket.

He ordered her to drive into the village of Whitegate. The post office is near the end of the street where they entered the village. He told her that she was to park outside while he went in and held up everyone in the post office and got the money. He tried to reassure her by telling her that she could always say he made her help him.

She was driving with Liam sitting beside her and Brendan in the back seat with the rifle. She drove as slowly as she could, trying to postpone everything for as long as she could.

Brendan saw from her actions that he could not trust her to stay outside in the car while he committed the robbery. He considered taking the keys with him while doing the robbery but realised that she would probably run for help with the child. If she got the word out, he would not be able to get very far before there would be a garda chase.

He tried to explain to her that there would be no danger to her and the child. He told her that the robbery would take a few minutes and that they would then go to Cork by driving north to Portumna, then across the Shannon into Tipperary, and then down the Tipperary side of the Shannon through Limerick and into Cork. He said that the guards would never figure out that this was their escape route.

She was adamant, in spite of her fear. He began cursing and swearing at her for not cooperating. He ducked down in the back seat whenever he saw a car passing.

Brendan finally told Imelda to drive past the post office, having realised that he could not make her follow his orders, even at the point of the gun.

Mae Tuohy had already delivered the money to the post office and started delivering the post to her route. She recognised Imelda's car coming towards her as she was getting ready to leave Whitegate. She saw Imelda making strange faces as she passed. It seemed that she was trying to signal that something was wrong. She could not understand what she was signalling.

Imelda reduced the speed of the car, hoping that Mae Tuohy would suspect that something was wrong. Mae Tuohy was surprised that Imelda did not stop to pick up her post. She saw the shape of someone in the back seat. Before the car sped away, Mae Tuohy was able to make out the features of someone resembling Brendan.

* * *

On Friday afternoon, Val Ballance returned to the house with Oisín, wondering why Imelda had not met him at the school for lunch. He saw that her Ford Fiesta was not parked in its usual place and wondered where she and Liam might be. He went into the house and found that they were not there.

The kettle was on the stove, the gas fire was on, and all of the water had boiled away. Val was also surprised that Imelda had left her tobacco pouch at the house as she always took it with her. He phoned two of Imelda's sisters who lived in Clare, to find out if they had heard from her.

On Saturday, Val Ballance became more concerned for Imelda and Liam. On Sunday, he went to the guards in Scariff and reported that they were missing.

* * *

Imelda drove erratically towards Woodford. When she got close to Woodford, she saw a woman and tried to signal to her for help. With Brendan in the back seat, she slowed down and moved her face as close to the windscreen as she could. She knew that she had drawn the attention of the woman driver coming towards her. She mouthed some words but could not talk.

Brendan saw what she was doing and shouted at her to speed up and not to try to give him away. He was afraid that she was about to stop the car, but he managed to scare her into continuing to drive and into speeding up.

In Woodford, he told her to drive towards Eyrecourt. They went through Portumna. Brendan was getting more agitated and confused because people seemed to have noticed that something was wrong. Near Eyrecourt, he became sure that a man saw them and felt that there was something strange. Liam was crying. Brendan could not prevent Imelda from trying to give signals to passing cars every chance she got.

He shouted at her to begin driving back to Cregg. He was now desperate. He complained that it was too late to go back and rob the post office, as most of the money would already have been picked up.

He complained that Imelda might have drawn enough attention to cause the guards to be called. He said that she had put him danger of spending years in jail, by not helping him to rob the post office.

For several hours, he made her drive around randomly as he kept changing his mind. He appeared to be getting waves of fear, talking incessantly about how the guards would soon be closing in. They stopped on the way to Cregg Wood to get groceries — especially, to get food for the child who was now crying a lot.

When they got close to Cregg, Brendan ordered Imelda to drive in the forest road. He wanted the car off the road as soon as possible. He believed that he had been seen by Mae Tuohy, and that she had recognised the car.

He wanted to use a more secondary road as soon as possible but found the first road off the primary forest road blocked.

The second road was open and he ordered Imelda to take the left turn. She drove a few hundred feet and then he told her to stop the car and get out with Liam. Brendan was now very frightened and seemed to be unable to stop talking.

She noticed the strange expressions on his face and knew that she was dealing with someone very dangerous and irrational. She tried to appease him but nothing would work.

Brendan ordered her to start walking into the wood with Liam. Sometimes Liam walked and sometimes she carried him. After walking for a long time, she wondered where they were going but she realised that Brendan was not sure either. He was now scared to release his hostages, believing that Imelda would do what his sister had done when she had escaped from him from the bedroom. After all, that was what had caused him to be in the most trouble.

If his sister had not gone to the dirt-bags, he would not have been made to go to court in Portumna. He would not have had to run away to England. He would not now have the guards chasing him, along with the British police. He had a similar problem now with Imelda Riney and her son.

Imelda insisted that they stop walking, that her son was tired, and that she was too tired to carry him any more. He continued to argue with her, insisting that she keep walking. He had the gun pointed at her and when she turned towards him, he would point it at her chest.

He was trying not to shout for fear of being heard and was constantly looking around as if expecting guards to move in at any time. He told her that she had to keep walking.

Suddenly, she stopped and told him that she would not go any further. She lunged at the gun pointed at her chest. He heard the shot and saw her thrown backwards to the ground. He looked at her for a while as if not sure what had happened. Then he saw her left eye where the bullet had entered her head. She was lying very still. He knew that she was dead.

Liam was standing close by and to Brendan's left. He was confused and frightened by the shot. He saw that there was something wrong with his mother and Brendan brought him over to her body.

Liam leaned over to look at his mother's face. He was calling her name. Brendan looked at the child's back and the dead body of the mother. He could not let the child live without his mother. He could not keep a witness to what had happened. He could not travel with the child.

He quietly removed the spent shell from the gun and put it in his pocket. He reloaded the gun, not wanting the child to look around and see what was about to happen.

He moved quietly towards the child who was still leaning over his mother. He fired a shot from very close range and watched Liam fall over on top of his mother and become very still.

He again removed the shell, put it in his pocket, and reloaded.

Brendan now had to act quickly. His own survival was now the only important thing. Getting to France would have to be postponed.

Hiding was all that mattered. He gathered up some branches and threw them over the bodies. There was silence everywhere. The quietness made him more aware of the thoughts flying around in his head.

He could hear his every move. He sometimes felt he could hear his thoughts talking back to him.

He knew that he had to leave Cregg Forest quickly. It no longer offered safety. It now offered only more danger. He could not remain close to the bodies.

None of his belongings, which were about a quarter of a mile away in another part of the wood, could be left this close to the bodies. The car could not be left nearby. The search would begin where the car was found. It had to be taken some distance from the bodies to put the searchers on the wrong trail.

Imelda and Liam had last been seen with him throughout the day and they had been seen with him by one person who knew him well — Mae Tuohy.

Val Ballance would be returning shortly with Oisín from school. He would wonder where Imelda was and where she had taken Liam. He might ask questions very soon and get a search started.

If he did, Mae Tuohy would remember what she had seen and tell the guards what she suspected.

He rushed back towards the road where the car was parked. The keys had been left in the ignition. He got into the car, started it, and began driving deeper into the wood along the main forest road. He would wait until dark before getting his tent and belongings.

Brendan found a safe place. He was tired and sleepy but his thoughts would not stop racing. He sometimes slept a dazed sleep as if everything was unreal. He tried to do what he had practised all of his life. He used his imagination to control fear.

He tried to stop feeling for Imelda Riney and Liam. He found that he could block out feelings and act as if something painful hadn't happened. This was now more of a struggle. It had become harder over the years.

The images, no matter how hard he tried, kept crowding in. This could be dangerous. He had to keep thinking, planning. He had to stop the images. He had to have plans. He had to keep moving.

Through the turmoil in his mind, some plans were forming. He always felt safe with his grandmother in Eyrecourt. She would help him, give him a place to stay, hide him, give him food, and give him clean clothing. He had to have clean clothing.

He would have to put his belongings in a safe place. He had to get rid of the car. When found, it would have to be free of all signs that he had ever been in it. And, above all else, it would have to be far away from the bodies.

When it was dark, he drove carefully to near where his tent and belongings were. He retrieved them, moving very quickly. He drove to where he could safely make a phone call, then called a friend and arranged to have him hold his belongings. The meeting and transfer were arranged very carefully.

Brendan knew that every minute in the car meant danger. He drove out a back road from the forest and through Woodford near Loughrea. He tried to remove the licence plates but he could not get them off. He finally got the front one off and threw it into a field.

He found an entrance to a forest and drove in. He got some petrol out of the tank and spilled it all over the interior of the car, lit a match and hoped that the flames and smoke would not be seen until the car was destroyed.

When he was sure that the car would be destroyed by the fire, Brendan began walking in the direction of his grandmother's house in Eyrecourt. He kept the gun hidden under his coat and made sure to carry the bag with the ammunition safely.

He had decided that if he were accosted by the guards, he would not be taken alive. He had enough ammunition to hold off an attack for a long time. He had counted the rounds several times. There were seventy or eighty rounds left.

He would have to concentrate on reloading quickly after each shot if he were in a shoot-out. He wouldn't mind dying in a shoot-out. He would master one kind of fear, the fear of dying. He would have the satisfaction of seeing others experience the fear he had felt all of his life.

15

Saturday 30 April
JJ Muggivan

After setting the car on fire, Brendan had begun walking towards Eyrecourt. He went to the house of Paddy Monaghan, his aunt's husband.

He arrived at the house and met Paddy Monaghan and his two sons. It was some time in the afternoon of Saturday 30 April. Brendan believed that, by this time, it would have been discovered that Imelda and Liam were missing. He still had the gun, the live ammunition, and the spent shells in his pocket. He had burned Imelda Riney's car and left it in a wood near Loughrea, having previously removed the bumper and front licence plate and thrown them into a field.

It was a long walk from the wood near Loughrea to Eyrecourt. But the Monaghans lived closer to where he was. He went there as he was hungry, and because he could not risk going to his grandparents' yet. His uncle, Mike Quinn, might show up and have a fight with him over not turning himself in to the guards as he had promised a month earlier.

Paddy Monaghan was his uncle by marriage. He was married to his mother's sister. There were three men in the family: Paddy Monaghan, the father, and John and Dermot Monaghan, the sons.

Brendan walked in, wearing a green cord jacket with jeans. He said that he had a gun to protect himself, but that he would not use it to kill or hurt anyone. It was about 3.30 or 4.00 on Saturday afternoon, 30 April.

Brendan had a meal with the Monaghans. They noticed that he became uneasy when he heard a garda car. He said that he had stolen a red Ford Fiesta and had burned it out in the forest. He told them that his fingerprints would have been in the car and he was afraid that the guards might be looking for him. He could see that the Monaghan men were uncomfortable with him and, anyway, he could not relax.

Later, the three men drove him to his grandparents' house, which was only a short walk away from the priest's house. As they drove, the gun was at Brendan's feet on the floor behind the driver's seat of the car.

When they got to his grandparents' house, Brendan put the gun around the back. While they were having tea with Mrs Quinn, he began to laugh for no apparent reason, and continued to laugh for about a quarter of hour. At the time, the Monaghans did not know about the disappearance of Imelda and Liam Riney.

Brendan was anxious to leave before his uncle returned. He had grown uneasy. After tea, he and the Monaghan brothers went outside where Brendan showed them the gun which he had put under a piece of polythene. The letters BSA were written on it.

The Monaghans walked down the road with Brendan towards Meelick and away from Eyrecourt. He told them that there was a shed up the road where he might spend the night. At one point, he stopped to put on his jacket and gave the gun to John Monaghan to hold.

16

Sunday 1 May

JJ Muggivan

After the Monghans had left Brendan, who said he was going to sleep in a hayshed, it seems that he went back to his grandmother's and she let him stay for the night. Mary Quinn did not want her family to know that she was helping him. Brendan now had no transportation again and he was becoming more desperate and panicky.

There were no other known sightings of Brendan until the following day. On Sunday 1 May, Margaret Maher visited her brother, Fr Joseph Walsh, with her children. It had not yet been reported that Imelda and Liam Riney were missing.

Fr Walsh knew Mary Quinn and brought Communion to her. He had mentioned Brendan to his sister on one occasion, when clothes had disappeared from his house. Brendan had known Fr Walsh's predecessors and had had access to the house in the past. On advice from the guards, the priest had had the locks changed. He had met Brendan at the baptism of Ann Marie's baby son for whom Brendan had stood as godfather, but other than that, he did not know him.

Margaret Maher noticed Brendan hovering around the rectory while Fr Walsh and the children were playing hurling. He didn't talk to them, but just stood staring. Fr Walsh's niece, Edel, said to her mother in a loud voice that there was 'a quare fella' watching them. Margaret Maher was embarrassed and told her daughter that she shouldn't blurt out something like that, as Brendan was a parishioner of Fr Joe's.

After the game, the priest brought his nieces and nephews for a drive. They stopped for ice-cream before heading home to Crosspatrick in County Kilkenny.

Little is known of Brendan's movements from Sunday afternoon, 1 May, until Ann Marie met him at their grandmother's house on Tuesday 3 May.

Brendan remained in the Eyrecourt area until late Tuesday night or early Wednesday morning. He had no transportation and hitch-hiking was now dangerous.

Ann Marie describes seeing her brother on Tuesday:

Just to comment briefly on the day I last had contact with Brendan [Tuesday 3 May 1994 in the afternoon], he was agitated, locking windows at my grandmother's house, opening doors, closing doors, and he was getting on my nerves as he continued to do this. I had a row or argument with him.

Later I became aware he had a gun and told him to go. He said he wasn't going to do anything to anyone that he only had it as protection. All I wanted him to do was leave the house as the gun was frightening me and so was he. He said, 'They're out there and they are coming.' I couldn't see anybody outside.

My grandparents and my son were also in the house at the time. He calmed down for a while and he ate a meal with me. Then he was just laughing at nothing and then he just left the house. I didn't know where he went nor did he say where he was going.

I returned later that evening to my flat in Portumna with my son. The next day I had a phone call from my grandmother saying there was some woman and a little boy missing in Whitegate. I told her I didn't know them at all as to which I didn't. After the phone call, the guards called to my flat and asked me was Brendan there. I said he wasn't and that they could look if they wanted to as I hadn't seen him since the evening before at my grandmother's house.

I sensed immediately that there was something wrong but I did not know what it was. I told the guards that he had a gun and watched the news all that day and later that evening went to my grandmother's house again. I didn't know what was going on.

I didn't really know Fr Walsh well as I lived in Portumna not Eyrecourt. He christened my son and that was the only contact I ever had with him as I already said during my evidence at the trial. Brendan also met Fr Walsh once and that was at my son's christening.

According to Ann Marie and her grandmother, Brendan did not return to the house again.

17

The Killing of
Fr Joseph Walsh —
A Reconstruction

JJ Muggivan

On Tuesday night, Brendan knew that he had to do
something desperate in order to escape from
Eyrecourt. He needed transportation. He had
heard that the news was out that they were searching for
Imelda and Liam Riney. He knew it wouldn't be long
before the guards were told they had last been seen with
him — and in her car. While the bodies were missing he
had time to act.

He felt unable to wait any longer for the guards to come
to his grandmother's house and start the shoot-out. He
was getting increasingly nervous, and decided to force the
priest, who lived a short distance away, to help him.

He decided to break into the priest's house, rob him
and take his car. He would have to find a way to convince

Fr Walsh not to raise the alarm until he was safely out of Eyrecourt.

Brendan watched until he saw Fr Walsh drive up. When he thought it was safe, he entered the house by the bathroom window, bringing the loaded .22 rifle with him. He left the bag with the ammunition outside.

No sooner was he inside, or part of the way in, than he found himself face to face with Fr Walsh. The priest asked him what he was doing. At first, Brendan was almost incoherent. He finally told Fr Walsh what he must do.

As the confrontation developed, Brendan became confused at Fr Walsh's reaction. The priest didn't appear frightened no matter how seriously Brendan talked.

Fr Walsh had heard about the missing mother and child and asked Brendan if he had had anything to do with them. He could tell by Brendan's reaction that he had hit a nerve and that he knew something.

Fr Walsh then told Brendan that he would not help him in any way until he told him where the missing people were. Brendan told him a story that he would continue using for the next several days.

He said that Imelda and Liam Riney were alive but were being held by another crowd in the Mountshannon–Whitegate area. Fr Walsh pushed him to tell him where he thought they were being held.

Brendan in desperation told the priest that they would be released safely at a later date. Fr Walsh said that he didn't believe this. Finally, Fr Walsh told Brendan he would help only if Brendan showed him where the missing people were being held.

Brendan now believed he had no choice and agreed to let Fr Walsh drive to Cregg Forest with him. He thought to himself that this would give him time to come up with a plan to get help from Fr Walsh without having to turn himself in to the guards.

In order to learn where the missing people were, Fr Walsh promised to help Brendan escape. Brendan agreed and both men got in the car to begin the drive to Cregg. The priest drove and Brendan was in the back seat with the gun. Before entering the car, he got his bag with the ammunition.

On the way, Fr Walsh tried to get as much information as he could from Brendan. Brendan was continuing to tell his story of the mother and child being held by another crowd. Fr Walsh did not believe this story but continued the journey to where Brendan said the people were.

The priest knew that the mother and child had been missing for several days and thought that they must be hungry and cold.

As they drove towards Portumna, Brendan was trying to think of a way to get help from Fr Walsh and avoid going to Cregg. They drove into Portumna and turned right when they reached the intersection of the Eyrecourt and Woodford roads.

To gain more time to think, Brendan told the priest to turn into a wood on the left-hand side of the road as they drove towards Woodford. Brendan wanted to avoid returning to where he had left the bodies of the mother and child.

The gate was locked and Fr Walsh told Brendan he did not believe that the missing people were in this area. Brendan agreed and told the priest to drive towards Cregg.

As they approached Cregg, Fr Walsh saw that Brendan was getting more and more agitated and nervous. However, he was able to persuade Brendan to continue the journey by agreeing to go to the bank in Banagher in the morning to get money for him to pay his way to France.

He promised not to raise any alarm until Brendan was safely away. He also promised to let Brendan have the car.

All he wanted in return was to be able to free the mother and child and end their family's worries and suffering.

At Brendan's direction, Fr Walsh turned right at Cregg Cross and drove into the forest. It was about 1 a.m. on Wednesday. Brendan was becoming more frightened at having to return to where the bodies were. He was trying not to show his fear because he didn't want the priest to suspect that the mother and child were dead.

He told Fr Walsh to turn left when they came to the secondary road where he had brought Imelda Riney and her son. When they were close to where he had entered the forest with the mother and child, Brendan told Fr Walsh to get out of the car with him.

It was very dark and Brendan began arguing that they would be unable to find the missing people at night. The headlights of the car could help only at the periphery of the wood.

Brendan tried to convince Fr Walsh that searching at night was a waste of time, but the priest did not want to give up. Finally, Fr Walsh suggested staying in the car for the night and, at dawn, making another attempt to go to where the people were. Fr Walsh had begun to suspect that the mother and child were not alive.

Brendan told Fr Walsh that they were close to a vacant house, Cregg House — the house where he was born. He told the priest to start driving out of the forest.

They got back into the car and left the forest. When they got to Cregg Cross, they took a right turn towards Cregg House. When they arrived at the entrance, Brendan got out and opened the gate into the field where the house was located.

There were no fences on the lane leading up to the house. Brendan closed the gate and got back into the car. The priest drove up the lane to the house and parked the car.

They both entered the rear section of the house and began to wait for the morning. Brendan was becoming even more agitated and began talking a lot to the priest. Fr Walsh encouraged him to keep talking and listened intently.

Brendan told him about his childhood, his mother, his incarcerations, his abuse, his stay with the Muggivans, his trips to England, and, in short, the story of his life. Several times, as Brendan talked about his mother's suicide attempts, and his own, he mentioned that he still wanted to die.

He put the gun in his mouth several times and talked about pulling the trigger and ending it all. He talked about the voices in his head that never seemed to stop. The priest persuaded him not to kill himself and told him he could be forgiven for anything but maybe not for death by his own hand.

The vigil continued throughout the night until it began slowly to get bright around 6 a.m. on Wednesday 4 May 1994. When it was bright enough, Fr Walsh said that it was time to go into the forest.

By now, Fr Walsh knew that they were looking for the bodies and that he would have to pray for them. He had the oils for the last rites in the car.

Both men left the house, with Brendan looking around carefully to make sure that there was no one nearby, especially squad cars. He was expecting guards to be searching. It was five days since Imelda and Liam Riney had gone missing so the search would be intense.

They drove back to the main road and turned left towards Cregg Cross. They turned into the forest and left again, on the road where Brendan had brought Imelda and Liam. Fr Walsh was driving.

They looked for an entrance to the forest where Brendan had entered with Imelda and Liam. They got out of the car several times. Brendan was getting increasingly worried that he wouldn't be able to find the entrance or the direction to the bodies. It was getting very bright and late in the morning.

Brendan finally thought he had found the point where he had entered with Imelda and Liam, and he and the priest walked into the wood through the trees.

He soon realised that they were not in the right place and that he would not be able to remember where to go. He began arguing with Fr Walsh that they were close enough to where the missing persons were.

He told the priest that they could not stay any longer, that he had to get away. He was now shouting at Fr Walsh to take him immediately to Banagher to get the money he needed to go to France.

The priest persisted in telling Brendan that they must continue searching until the mother and child were found.

Brendan suddenly told him that there was no hurry in finding them — they were dead. Fr Walsh pleaded that it wouldn't be right to leave them without giving them the last rites and asked Brendan please to continue with the search. But Brendan was in a hurry.

The priest knelt down in front of a rock and started saying the rosary. Brendan asked him to pray for Imelda Riney and Liam. As the priest said the rosary, Brendan thought to himself that he intended to say the entire rosary and there certainly was no time for that — the guards might already be entering the forest. He needed the priest's car.

Fr Walsh was kneeling with his back to Brendan. Brendan moved closer and pointed the gun at the back of the priest's head, then pulled the trigger.

He ran back to the car, making sure to remove the shell casing from the gun and put it in his pocket. Finding the keys left in the car, he started the engine and drove in the direction the car was facing, coming to a dead end.

He turned the car around and rushed from the forest, keeping an eye out for anyone who might witness him leaving. It was still early and there was little traffic on the road as he drove to Portumna.

He blindly drove the route he had planned to drive with Imelda and Liam. He went to Portumna and across the Shannon into Tipperary. He was heading in the direction of Limerick but did not want to go there, and slowly realised that he was driving around aimlessly.

18

The Search Begins

Tony Muggivan

Word spread fast throughout Whitegate and Mountshannon. On Sunday night, I had heard the news in Cologne, Germany, that Imelda Riney and her youngest son were missing. I called JJ and we talked about calling the guards. I immediately connected the disappearance of the Rineys to Brendan as I knew he was back in the Mountshannon and Whitegate area.

We did not know yet if the guards had been contacted but later found out that Val Ballance had contacted them. JJ believed that the Rineys were already dead. I could not accept this. He asked me not to share his belief but to do all I could to make people take the report seriously.

I was very anxious to get home but the soonest I could leave was Tuesday 3 May. We started from Cologne on Tuesday, very early in the morning. My friend, Hans, was driving as I wasn't used to driving on the right-hand side of the road.

We drove from Germany into Belgium and then to Le Havre in France where we caught the ferry to Dover. We all found the journey long as we didn't have any communication with Mountshannon, and we continued to worry about the missing mother and child.

When we arrived in Dover, I took over the driving and drove to Swansea in Wales where we caught the ferry for Cork. We boarded the ferry for the ten-hour overnight trip to Cork on Tuesday evening and tried to settle down for a few hours of sleep.

We had a little food on the ferry and then the storm hit. Mary and Hans got very sick. In all the years I had fished with Hans, in all kinds of weather, I had never seen him sick before.

It is now strange to imagine Fr Walsh and Brendan in Cregg House as we were crossing on the ferry from Swansea to Cork. It is even stranger to realise that the curate had probably been killed an hour or two before we docked in Cork.

It was a bad storm and it made us two hours late coming into Cork. We arrived in Cork at about eight o'clock on Wednesday morning and stopped for a cup of tea and a quick couple of slices of toast as none of us felt very well after the night we had had.

I drove the hundred miles to Mountshannon. I was driving Hans's Mercedes and I travelled at very high speed without any complaints from Hans or Mary. We were in a hurry to get to Mountshannon to see if we could help in the search.

As I was driving, I was thinking of what I would have to do. I asked myself what Mary would think when she saw me loading a gun and taking it with me on the search. What would my children think? I hoped to God they had

143

him caught. If I came across him and he had a gun and the people were not found, what would I do?

I had a heavy box strapped to the roof of the car and, with the wind and sharp turns, I had to slow down as I got nearer to Mountshannon.

I was remembering my efforts to have Brendan hospitalised five years earlier and I was continuing to ask why they hadn't admitted him for treatment. I did not yet realise that they had since admitted him after he had tried to kill his sister and her baby with a knife, but had released him after a couple of weeks.

The questions were racing around in my mind, one after the other. Why did he come back from England? Why didn't he come to see me when he came back and give me a chance to help him again?

So many questions. What was I going to do when I got home if I found him and he had a gun? How was I going to search for a man who was a good shot with a gun and who knew his way around the fields, mountains, and forests of the area as well as I did? What would happen if I shot him and we never found where he had hidden Imelda and Liam?

If he saw a guard with me, he would shoot for certain. Questions, questions, questions — nothing only questions — no answers. I decided that I would go searching alone for a while and give him a chance to approach me.

Finally, we got home with none of us feeling very well. I loaded a double-barrel shotgun for Hans and brought him to his house on the Hill of Dooras, thinking to myself that Brendan knew every nook and cranny of the area and knew exactly the layout of Hans's house.

I heard the report that Fr Walsh had not shown up for Mass that morning. I realised that there were now three people missing — Imelda Riney, Liam Riney and Fr Walsh.

Hans showed no surprise at my giving him the gun and he seemed ready to use it if he had to. I warned him to keep the gun close by at all times, to keep his doors locked, not to get into a conversation with Brendan if he came to his house, and to shoot him in the legs if he tried to break in.

I was worried for Hans because Brendan had worked for him before. Hans was a very kind man. He had paid him well, but had always paid him from his wallet where he would have had a large amount of cash. Brendan would have remembered this. Hans also had a good car, a Mercedes 250, which Brendan would probably have liked to have.

I went back to my own home — two miles away — and loaded my wife's brother's gun for Mary. Her brother, Michael O'Sullivan, was away at the time. I gave her the same instructions.

I loaded my own gun and put it into the boot of the car. Before I left, Mary gave me some clothing for the mother and child as she was worried that they would be cold and wet if they had been out in the weather since they had gone missing.

I set off alone. It was now about the middle of the afternoon. I began my search with all the empty holiday homes in the area. I would drive slowly up to each house, as close as I could, and search for signs of footprints, broken windows, or anything that would show me that someone was there. It was slow work but I searched most of the obvious houses and got home before dark.

I thought it too dangerous to approach houses where he might be hiding as he would have a chance to see me without my being able to see him first. I had my mind made up that, should the situation arise, I would shoot him. My reasons for this decision were my contact with my brother and his advice, and Brendan's threat in 1991 to 'get' someone close to me.

I went to Whitegate first thing on Thursday morning, 5 May. There seemed to be about a hundred people there and two guards. Most of the people were friends of Imelda Riney's and of her children and were not originally from the area.

I asked the guards to close all of the roads but they said that they didn't think there was enough manpower available yet. It was sad to see the worry on the faces of the missing people's friends. It was already known that a priest from Eyrecourt was also missing. Fr Joseph Walsh lived only a short distance from Mary Quinn, Brendan's grandmoter.

For reasons not known to me, the search was called off. I continued on my own, searching the empty houses and the forest roads. I spent all day searching but saw no sign of him or the missing people anywhere.

I saw one garda squad car but I was reluctant to get involved with the guards, mostly because Brendan hated them and had told me in 1991 that should the opportunity arise, he would, as he said it, 'do one in'.

I didn't see anyone else searching but I knew that the alarm had already been raised and that there was probably a search going on.

At dark, I came home. My son's gun was at home during this time. I wanted Mary to stay indoors and use the gun if she had to.

That night, I kept the gun near me at all times. Later, I heard from locals that there was a widespread search planned for the following day. The search was to start the following morning from Whitegate Church, which is not far from where Imelda Riney and her child lived.

That night also, Denis Woods came to the house and offered to join me in searching in the morning.

19

Killer at Large

Tony Muggivan

On Friday morning, 6 May, Denis Woods and I started searching again. We warned some people to go home and stay indoors until it was over. At one point, Denis Woods asked me what we would do if we met Brendan and he had a gun. I told him that I had a loaded shotgun in the boot and that, if we met him in a car, I would try to ram him with my car.

We now knew that Fr Walsh's car had been found burned out and hanging over the edge of Williamstown Pier. We drove to Williamstown and saw the burned-out car.

Brendan had tried to drive or push it over the edge. The car had got straddled when the front wheels went off the edge. I think it was a front-wheel drive and lost traction when the front wheels were off the ground. It seemed like a suicide attempt. Knowing Brendan, I thought that it might have been a fake attempt to distract pursuers, or an attempt to destroy evidence.

The water was deep enough and dark enough to keep a car from being found for a very long time. The car was found close to where Brendan's friend had been drowned a year and a half earlier.

We began travelling all of the back roads. The back roads are very rough so the driving was slow. We met one woman cutting waste timber on the edge of the forest. We stopped the car and Denis advised her to go home as Brendan could harm her.

She said that she had her saw to protect her. Denis told her that the saw wouldn't be a lot of help to her and that she would be better off to go home and stay in the house. She saw that Denis was serious and she followed his advice. We met another couple out for a walk and gave them the same advice.

We arrived home for food about 2 p.m. and, while we were eating, the guards phoned and asked me to help find Brendan. They offered to come to my house but I told them that I would prefer to meet in the garda station at about 3.30 p.m.

I went to Scariff garda station and told them that I had searched all the holiday houses and had seen no sign that Brendan had been in any of them. I told them that Denis Woods and I had also been searching all day and that the only place we hadn't searched was the forest around Cregg.

I said that Brendan talked a lot about this area. I noticed that they had very clear maps of the entire area around Whitegate and Mountshannon. The officer in charge asked me to look at the map and show them the area I was talking about. I did this and pointed to the Cregg area. He asked me if I would go to Cregg Wood with two guards and show them the area. They took me in a squad car to where I had pointed out on the map.

As we drove, I began to feel more certain that Cregg Wood was the best place to continue searching. I remembered Brendan telling me about a deer which he would often see in the field around his old family home. I also remembered that that it was in Cregg that he had burned Denis Tirnan's car a number of years previously.

I directed the guard driving the car to go straight into the forest at Cregg Cross. On the way in, we passed a number of side roads before coming to one in particular.

At the entrance to this road, we turned left into the forest in the direction of Brendan's old family home. The road was short and came to a dead end.

At the end of it, it was possible to walk a short distance through a part of the forest, and through a field or two, and come to Brendan's original family home.

At the entrance to this short road, there was a dead pine tree partly blocking the entrance. We stopped the car at this spot. I did not know yet that we were within a few hundred yards of Brendan's victims.

There were marks on the dead tree which showed that someone had driven a car over it. I said that no local driver would risk damaging a car by driving over the tree and that the person who had driven over it must have been in a great hurry.

There was a clear tyre track of a small car and some of the bark was stripped off the branch. I immediately believed that we had found the first tracks of Brendan and that this was where the search should be focused.

We removed the tree and drove in the side road about a hundred yards. We stopped and found more tyre tracks going all the way to the end of the road where there was a circular clearance for turning around.

As we searched around for signs, I shuddered when I looked and saw one guard about twenty yards away from me and realised that he had no gun. If the other guard had one, it was hidden. I remember saying to myself, 'My God, if Brendan is around, we are all sitting ducks.'

I had a sudden, intense fear that we were in danger and that Brendan could be very close by.

I started to walk towards the guards when one of them said we should return to Scarriff and immediately arrange for a big search of the area. The full search was arranged for early the following morning, Saturday 7 May 1994. It was getting dark in the forest and it was very silent. I was glad to get out of there.

That night, my oldest son, Brendan, came home from Dublin. I felt a bit more secure. Everyone was in bed by midnight but I stayed up thinking about what to do next.

Brendan O'Donnell had not been seen by anyone that we knew of for over a week. The Rineys had not been seen since the previous Friday. Fr Walsh had not been seen since close to midnight on Tuesday night.

I stayed up all night and was in constant contact with Killaloe garda station.

I was wondering what Brendan was doing for food. I hadn't heard of any car being stolen or of a break-in at any house. As there had been no report of a stolen car since Fr Walsh's car had been found, it was likely that Brendan was on foot and probably looking for a car.

I phoned my brother several times and we talked of precautions. Like JJ, I was now convinced that we were searching for bodies and that Brendan was now more dangerous that ever.

Until now, I had never been sure that he might shoot me. But if he had killed his hostages, killing others would be likely if he needed to escape or get away. I believed that we were very close to the end of the search and that something significant was about to happen.

Having fastened all of the windows and turned off all the lights, I sat in the front room with the loaded shotgun in my hand. I didn't have the dog any more. He was a good watchdog but he had died of old age. I remembered him barking the night Brendan had first come to my home.

I was listening carefully for sounds. I had never realised before how many sounds there are in a house with a family, but I had never previously listened so intently, or for so long.

I was very tired, having had almost no sleep since leaving Cologne on Tuesday. It was now Friday night and I was anxious to stay awake. I was afraid to lie down on the bed in case I would fall asleep.

I remembered the threatening phone call I had got years before. I remembered the guard telling me that Brendan would get me for having set him up to be arrested in my home.

My thoughts were suddenly disturbed by the sound of the phone. It was five minutes past one o'clock. The sound frightened the life out of me. I was sitting on the floor right beside the phone in the front room, as there are a lot of glass windows in that room.

I picked up the phone and said 'Hello' a couple of times. There was no response and no tones to put money in the box as there would have been if the call had been from a payphone. Then it went dead.

I wondered if Brendan had rung to see if I was home or to ask me to drive him out of the area. I called the guards in Killaloe and told them about the phone call. I told them of my belief that Brendan might make an attempt to get me to help him escape.

The guard who answered told me that they had my house under constant observation as they also expected that Brendan might make an effort to come to my home. He told me to be careful as all roads out of the area were closed and there was a lot of fire power out.

I assured him that I would not cooperate with Brendan in any way but wanted to have a plan in case he overpowered me. We made arrangements regarding what I should do if I were taken hostage. I described my car and told him that it was a left-hand drive. I told him that if I was driving, I would have four headlamps on, and if Brendan was driving, there would be only two lights on.

I believed that Brendan would not know about pulling the switch further out in order to put the four lights on. If there was shooting, I wanted the guards to know which side of the car to fire at.

The guard said that he would give this information to the guards on the roads. Just over an hour later, at 3.30 a.m. to be exact, I saw the lights of a car driving on the road a couple of hundred yards from the house.

I called the guards again and they told me that they had decided to be visible around my house. They told me not to worry. That didn't help much.

Mary got up at about six o'clock and I lay down for a while. I dropped off to sleep. Mary called me at about seven and told me that Brendan had been spotted in the Whitegate area and that there was a guard in the kitchen wanting me to talk to him if contact was made. In case he put up resistance, the guards wanted me to try to persuade him to give himself up.

Mary told me that she would have a cup of tea ready as soon as I got up. The guard's name was P.J. Higgins. I had known him for many years as he had once been stationed in Mountshannon.

He told me where the sighting had been and I was familiar with the area. I drove my own car to the place known as O'Donnell's Cross. There were guards with guns everywhere. They showed me where he had been seen.

I went down a small road and started crossing through some fields, hoping to come on his tracks. I tried to stay as close as possible to stone fences. The guards had told me that there was no report of Brendan having a gun and that there were no reports of a stolen gun in the area. This didn't mean very much as most people don't check their guns very often.

My head was throbbing from lack of sleep and my stomach was paining me with nerves. I got over a fence and into a field where there were sheep. I noticed that all the sheep were lying down and jumped up when they heard or saw me. I said to myself that if someone had been here earlier, the sheep wouldn't be lying down as they are very alert and wary animals. Cattle will remain lying down, looking at a person with curiosity, but sheep will usually run all over the place.

There was a fresh drain with soft ground on each side. I went along this for a while but saw no tracks anywhere. I started back for O'Donnell's Cross as I saw a helicopter circle overhead and suddenly take off in one direction. I believed that Brendan had been sighted again somewhere else.

I hurried back at a run and saw a number of guards listening to the radio in a squad car. One guard told me that Brendan had taken Fiona Sampson hostage and that he had a car.

I went up on high ground with two guards but could see no sign of anything in the surrounding mountain area.

At that moment, a report came in that the car had been sighted. It was crashed and abandoned on the mountain road leading into Woodford in County Galway. I knew exactly where it was as it was near my mother's family home. I had my own car and wondered for a while if I should take a short cut through the forest to the location of the crashed car. I decided against it since parts of the road were very bad and washed away from flooding. If I got bogged down, I could be stuck for hours.

I told the guards to follow me as they were not familiar with the area. We were there in about fifteen minutes. We had some delay as we met a timber lorry some distance from the crashed car.

We could see the helicopter circling in the distance. When we got to where the helicopter was, I asked a guard if they had seen Brendan. He said that Brendan was gone and still had Fiona Sampson.

This was the first time I lost my temper and, for a while, was verbally abusive to some guards. I now realise that this was completely out of order. At the time, I was angry because it seemed that the search was concentrated on the mountain, and entry to a nearby forest was still possible for Brendan. I believed that if he got into the forest, he would be free for days, or even weeks.

Not much later, news came in that Brendan had been captured and that his hostages, Fiona Sampson and Eddie Cleary, were safe.

20

More Hostages

JJ Muggivan

———————————

At the trial, Fiona Sampson gave evidence of her experiences on the morning of 7 May 1994.

She was still in bed when, at 7.45, she heard glass breaking. She got up to investigate and saw a man with a gun coming into the kitchen through the back door. He had tights over his face and was wearing a green jacket and dark clothing. Her first instinct was to go into a bedroom and close the door behind her, but she decided that there was no point in doing that, and returned to the hallway, where she recognised the man as Brendan O'Donnell, whom she knew as an acquaintance because he lived locally and they had been to school together.

They greeted each other and he told her he needed to get out of the area. They went into the kitchen together where he saw the car keys and asked her if she could drive. When she told him that she could, he pointed the gun at her and she felt she had no choice. She asked if she could put on shoes and change her clothes because she was dressed only in a night dress, but he wouldn't allow her to, insisting that they had to leave immediately.

Fiona drove away from the farm, with Brendan in the passenger seat, pointing the gun at her. They drove in the direction of Williamstown Pier, and Brendan complained that they weren't going fast enough. At one point, he asked her to stop, and he got out and into the back of the car, and then told her to continue driving. From time to time, he lifted the stocking from his face.

In the course of the journey, Fiona Sampson engaged Brendan in a number of conversations, at one stage discussing the relative merits of male and female drivers. She knew that Brendan was being sought, and she asked him on three occasions about the disappearances of Imelda and Liam Riney and Fr Walsh. He said that he knew where Imelda and Liam were and that they were safe, although he hadn't seen them since he had got a lift from Imelda the previous Friday week. He denied any knowledge of Fr Walsh but was worried that he would be connected with the disappearance.

Brendan told Fiona that he had slept out the previous night and hadn't eaten in days. He said that he wouldn't kill or rape her and that she could go as soon as he was out of the area. However, at another stage in the journey, he told her that he would kill her if he had to, as he had nothing to lose by it, but that it would be quick. She told him that she wasn't prepared to die yet.

Having found a denim jacket in the back of the car, Brendan passed it to Fiona to put on, telling her to keep driving while she was doing so. However, she lost control of the car which went into a spin and off the road. Brendan was angry and accused her of crashing it deliberately, but she told him that if she had planned to crash the car, she would have done it on the main road.

156

Neither Fiona nor Brendan succeeded in getting the car back onto the road, and Brendan attempted to set fire to it, telling Fiona that he would get a bigger one. He then ordered her to set off on foot with him across bog and rough terrain. She was now wearing the denim jacket and her mother's coat which had also been in the car, but she was still barefoot.

There was a helicopter above as they left the car, and Brendan told her to turn the coat inside out, explaining that the dark green lining would be less obvious than the outer purple colour. He asked her what height she was and wanted to know if she had any metal on her. He said that the helicopter would have an infra-red scan which would be able to detect metal from a distance and that it would also have long-range guns which would not be able to tell the difference between them.

Fiona's thighs were badly scratched and there were stones and thorns in her feet. At one point, Brendan stopped to inspect the soles of her feet for blood, explaining that if there were dogs out after him, they would pick up the scent.

There was a car outside a house they came to, but Brendan said that it was too old and wouldn't move fast enough. At another house, the owner was standing at an upstairs window with a gun and ordered them off his property and fired a shot in the air. Brendan threatened to come back or to send someone else back to get the man.

At another house, the owner was inside, drinking tea. When they went to the window, he told them that he had no car. Brendan checked the sheds but, finding no car, left. Still on foot, they headed off in the direction of Woodford.

When Brendan saw a navy Golf car approaching them, he flagged it down and ordered the driver at gunpoint to let them in. Fiona was forced to get into the back with

Brendan. Her memory after that was vague but she remembered Brendan telling the man to drive down the road and turn, and that he had the gun pointing towards the front of the car. She noticed people with guns coming towards the car and said she heard a shot being fired and saw the barrel of the gun being shoved from left to right.

There was a lot of activity, and Brendan was arrested. Fiona was lifted by guards from the back of the car.

* * *

Fiona Sampson's testimony provided a remarkable account of a desperate man, on the run and willing to engage in any activity to avoid capture. She was led to believe that her abduction was solely for the purpose of escaping the manhunt.

Her testimony, together with those of Eddie Cleary, Andreas Hannefield and Kevin Mooney provided substantial information about Brendan's state of mind as he took and held hostages. Escaping from the guards appears to have been his sole motivation.

There are three instances in the entire saga of Brendan O'Donnell where we get to see him through the eyes of one of his hostages — that is, through the eyes of an abducted individual in danger of being killed.

The three instances are when he held his sister and nephew hostage, when he held Fiona Sampson hostage, and when he held Eddie Cleary hostage. Three hostages died and four survived.

Only one of these instances was clearly inspired by a paranoid belief — namely, the holding of Ann Marie hostage. Brendan had the delusional belief that his sister was planning to put poison in his milk.

However, this action, occurring out of a paranoid belief, set in motion the chain of events that led to his going on the run from the Garda Síochána in Ireland and the police in England. His goal, after the assault on his sister, was to run from imprisonment, which was a real danger. His early imprisonment had involved painful events, one of which was probably rape.

Brendan's abduction of Fiona Sampson and Eddie Cleary, and his attempted taking of cars from Andreas Hannefield and Kevin Mooney, were inspired purely by his need to escape the real — not imagined — danger of being captured again and imprisoned. Killing any of these four individuals would have been done mainly to facilitate escape.

In the past, Brendan would simply have stolen these people's cars, but the circumstances were different now. There was greater urgency and he believed that pursuit by police was imminent.

Taking Imelda Riney's car, even if he could have robbed the post office by himself, would have carried the risk of Imelda's calling the police as soon as he had left her house. In other words, his hostages became dangerous to him. Brendan Muggivan discovered early that Brendan O'Donnell had learned at a young age to destroy or hide evidence of his wrongdoing.

Was killing ever a primary motivation for what Brendan did? Could he have been planning to take Imelda Riney and Liam deep into Cregg Forest and leave them there in the hope that they wouldn't be able to find their way out — or to the guards — until he was safely out of the area?

Once the theory that the abductions were not motivated for the satisfaction of committing cold-blooded killings is left out of the picture, Brendan O'Donnell's behaviour begins to make more sense.

I believe that the abduction of Imelda Riney and Liam, and the abduction of Fr Walsh, were for the same purposes as the abductions of Fiona Sampson and Eddie Cleary.

After the bodies had been found, Tony Muggivan told a friend of his, Bridget (B. Mae) Dinan, what had happened. When she heard the account, she said to Tony, 'Sure the craytur wouldn't have done it if he could stop himself.' He was known to have been out of control of himself for a long time.

The testimony of Fiona Sampson, Eddie Cleary, Andreas Hannefield and Kevin Mooney made it virtually impossible for Brendan's legal defence team to sustain a defence of not guilty by reason of the kind of insanity associated with Hebephrenic or Disorganized Schizophrenia.

Delusional Disorder, Paranoid Type, untreated can be a devastating mental-health disorder, but it can also be a deceptive disorder as an individual can frequently appear very rational and normal. Brendan ranged back and forth between the florid symptoms of the disorder and a deceptive appearance of normality.

He was acting on a paranoid belief when he took his sister hostage. When she survived, he was in danger, and the danger presented itself immediately — she went to the guards, he was arrested, hospitalised briefly, released from hospital, and charged with a crime.

The chain of events leading to these tragedies started with his having acted on a paranoid belief. This chain of events ended with a real — and 'rationally' planned — struggle to escape what was now a real danger.

This pattern was present throughout his life. He would engage in impulsive behaviour that would put him in conflict with police. If he did not receive help immediately to extricate himself with a reasonable or rational solution, he would make matters worse.

Brendan's experience of Tony having previously helped to extricate him from problems led him to attempt contact with Tony immediately before the abduction of Imelda Riney. Tony's unavailability left him to his own devices.

And when left to his own devices he engaged in disastrous problem-solving. As he said to Tony after his capture, 'I fucked up this time.'

* * *

It was the morning of 7 May 1994. Andreas Hannefeld was at home on his farm in Woodford, County Galway. He and his wife had heard on the radio about the people who had disappeared. He made sure that his shotgun was handy, and he told his family to go upstairs.

Andreas was keeping watch at the front window when he saw Brendan and Fiona coming towards the farm gate. He did not recognise them, and he dialled 999 to report what he had seen. He watched as the strangers came through the fields, taking cover by the trees. It took them about five minutes to get as far as the second gate, at the house.

Brendan and Fiona stopped, and Andreas shouted from the upstairs window. 'Fuck off, you stupid idiot,' he roared.

Brendan replied that he only wanted a car, but Andreas told him that his wife had the keys and was not there, to which Brendan replied that if Andreas did not get the key, he would come back later, or send somebody else back to kill him.

Andreas loaded his shotgun and fired a shot in the air, away from Brendan and Fiona.

Brendan became very agitated and shouted, 'Fuck you, you English bastard or whatever you are.' Then he and Fiona left. Andreas again phoned the guards.

Kevin Mooney lived about half a mile from the Hannefelds. At about 9.30 a.m., he saw Brendan and Fiona outside his house. He did not know them, and he locked the door.

Brendan asked if he had a car and he told him he did not. Brendan put a rifle to the window, but then went off towards Woodford.

Eddie Cleary was driving his car on a quiet country road near Woodford, when he turned a bend and was confronted by a man pointing a gun at him. There was a girl beside him.

Brendan shouted at Eddie to stop the car or he would blow his head off. Eddie stopped the car and thought of reversing back down the road, but could tell from Brendan's mood that he would shoot him dead if he tried that.

Brendan asked Eddie if he was 'a cop'. Eddie assured him that he was not and appealed to him not to shoot anyone. Brendan, who was holding the gun to Fiona's shoulder, tried to open the car door but they were all locked.

Eddie got out of the car and saw a garda car behind and guards in the ditch beside the road.

One of the guards shouted, 'Give up, O'Donnell. You're surrounded' and a warning shot was fired.

Putting the gun to Fiona's head, Brendan shouted at the guards, 'Back off to fuck now or I'll blow her fucking head off!' Then he pushed Fiona into the back of the car and got in beside her. He told Eddie to drive.

With the gun to the back of his head, Eddie drove a few yards. There were more garda cars in front of them and the road was blocked. Brendan told him to turn the car, but as Eddie did so, he manoeuvred badly to give the guards a chance to reach them.

Brendan, who was very agitated and shouting at Eddie to 'turn the fucking car', fired a shot through the roof. Eddie could see that the guards were beside the car at this stage. He grabbed the barrel of the gun and held it for a few moments, then he pulled the gun from Brendan and put it in the passenger seat beside him.

A guard came up to the window beside Fiona and she unlocked the door. He lifted her out. Eddie would testify at the trial that Fiona was 'terribly distressed' at this point, and in a 'shocking condition.' He would also recall that when Brendan was lying on the ground, his words were 'I'm fucked now.'

Throughout his ordeal, Eddie Cleary expected that Brendan might shoot him at any moment.

21

Under Arrest

Tony Muggivan

After word had come in that Brendan had been captured and that Fiona Sampson was safe, I went to where the arrest had been made and was told that a senior officer wanted to talk to me.

When I found him, he asked me to go to Loughrea barracks because there was a possibility that Brendan would talk to me and give me information about the mother, the child, and the priest. He offered to bring me to Loughrea, which was about fifteen miles away, in a squad car. I decided to travel in my own car.

I was brought to see Brendan very soon after I arrived in Loughrea. This was only a short time after his arrest. I hadn't seen him in about two years, except briefly in a passing car a few weeks earlier.

I was left alone with him in a room on the second level of the building. We shook hands and I started talking to him very calmly.

One of the first things he asked me was if I could get a gun in to him. He asked me if I had been searched coming in. I told him I had been searched and there was no way I could get him a gun. I asked him what he would want a gun for. He replied that he could take a couple of the cunts — meaning guards — with him in a shoot-out.

I said, 'Brendan, there is no chance. Look out the window — there's an armed soldier right outside.' I asked him about the missing people and he said that he had nothing to do with them but there was a gang up around there and they had them.

He went on to say that he could have shot Fiona Sampson if he had wanted to. He said that 'the little cunt only held him up and never stopped complaining'. He went on and on about the gun, saying that it wasn't worth a fuck since it was only a single shot.

He told me that his feet were sore and hurting him and that he needed a basin of warm water to soak them. He had no shoes or socks and his feet looked bloodless. I noticed that he had no scratches on his face, hands, or anywhere I could see.

I asked for approval to call my brother in New Orleans and was taken to a room where several officers were sitting around a table talking. I gave JJ a description of Brendan and told him how he had responded to me.

I told him how Brendan would talk about everything but the missing people — for example, another gang, his feet, the guards and how they were out to get him. He saw himself as the victim, and not the missing people.

JJ told me that if I talked to Brendan again to address him as if he had multiple personalities — even though he didn't — and to watch for signs in his eyes or on his face of what he was hiding when I asked certain questions. He told me that he would have a unique response if I asked him a direct question close to the truth. The plan was to state my belief that the people were dead and that it was wrong to keep the bodies from the families.

Brendan started talking about the guards, and how they were out to get him, and he kept talking about them and cursing them. I got impatient and angry and I shouted, 'Fuck the fucking guards. What do they have to do with the missing people?'

The guards outside the door heard my shouting and one of them looked in. He left and closed the door. Whenever I tried to get him talking about the missing people, Brendan would only talk about how the guards were out to get him.

I realised that I wasn't going to get the information I was looking for by pleading. I finally ignored his explanations about who was holding the missing people, and about gangs in the area.

I suddenly said to him, catching him off guard, 'I don't want you to tell me where they are. I know where they are. They're in Cregg Forest and I will find them.'

He was startled by the suddenness of my statement and, before he had time to think, he said, 'No, they're not.' I asked him if they were alive, and he said he had nothing to do with them.

I immediately knew that I had the answer — the bodies were in Cregg Forest. I noticed that he did not say that the people were alive, but said, instead, he had nothing to do with them.

I did not press him any further and he became quiet. A solicitor came in and I left. I told a guard about his request for a basin of water. Before I left, I asked Brendan if there was anyone he wanted to talk to.

I told him that there was a guard from Clare downstairs and he said he would like to talk to him. I passed this information on.

I left the room and met the guard from Clare. His name was G.T. Kelly. Our conversation was about returning to Cregg Forest and arranging the search for the missing people. I told Garda Kelly that Brendan's response to my statement that I knew the missing people were in Cregg Forest confirmed what we had concluded from the tyre marks on the Cregg Forest road and on the dead tree.

I agreed to meet them at a particular place near Cregg Forest at three o'clock. With that, another officer gave us a cup of tea and some biscuits. I thanked her as I hadn't eaten since seven o'clock that morning — it felt like a week since then.

I had run and walked so much that my clothes were stuck to me with sweat and my feet were sore as there had been water in my shoes since early in the morning.

I left the Loughrea barracks by the back door. A guard told me that there was a big crowd at the front entrance, and many reporters. I went down a side road and as I had a cousin living nearby, and as I had some time before the meeting with the guards back in Clare, I went to visit her for a few minutes. I chatted with my cousin who also knew Brendan as she had met him several times while visiting my home.

She made some tea and sandwiches for me and after I had eaten them, I started for home about twenty-seven miles away. I arrived home at about two o'clock and changed my clothes. Mary was relieved at the news that Brendan had been caught and told me that the Killaloe guards had been calling her regularly prior to the arrest, advising her to be watchful.

I left for the meeting at Cregg at about 2.30 p.m. as I wanted to visit my wife's uncle, Son O'Donnell, for a few minutes. He was very agitated over the missing people having known Imelda Riney well as she lived only a very short distance from his house.

When I got there, he started to cry and said, 'They're all dead.' I tried to calm him as he had a very bad heart and was in very bad health. He told me about having met Brendan about a week before Imelda and her child went missing and having told him to stay away from her and her children.

When I got to Cregg Forest, there was a crowd of people spread out searching the area. I recognised many of my neighbours and family members — Patsy Donnellan, John Donnellan, Brendan Muggivan, Vera O'Rourke, Joe O'Rourke and Liam Pearl, the man who eventually found the Rineys.

I would have preferred to have started searching where the two guards and I had found the tyre marks the previous evening. However, I said nothing as I thought we could go in a line and reach that area fairly quickly. I suggested we look up into the trees. I didn't know what to expect but was thinking that Brendan was capable of using a rope and pulling his victims up into the trees. I believed he wouldn't have had a shovel to bury them.

After a while, I got off on my own and ran into very dense forest with a lot of low-lying bramble. I remembered that Brendan had had no marks on his hands or face and realised that he, more than likely, had not come this way. I came out on another road in the forest and made my way back to the central point of activity. When I got there, I was asked to take some guards to some empty houses some miles away. I said I would but I asked that two men who were very familiar with the forest, Joe Duffy and Denis Woods, be contacted and asked to join in the search of the forest. Cregg Wood, like all forests planted by Coillte, the state forestry agency, had been planted to a plan. As Denis had worked at the forest for many years and Joe Duffy was an inspector with Coillte, both had an excellent knowledge of the area.

I left in a squad car and we searched some empty houses. On our way back through the village of Mountshannon, Joe O'Rourke stopped us and told us that Fr Walsh's body had been found. We drove on to Cregg and I was surprised how close Garda Meehan, Garda Higgins and I had been to his body when we found the tyre marks.

Denis Woods, who had found Fr Walsh's body, came over to me and said, 'It's going to be the same for Imelda Riney and her child.'

I came home and told my wife and family the news. I called JJ in New Orleans and we both wondered why all the bodies had not been found together. However, we both felt that the other bodies must be nearby.

My wife, my family and I talked into the night, remembering all that had happened over the previous five years and how we had been unable to get the necessary help which might have prevented such a tragedy.

* * *

The guards had arranged to return to the search for Imelda Riney and her child next morning, Sunday morning. I joined a group of one guard and seven or eight locals. I was waiting to go into the forest near where Fr Walsh's body had been found. We didn't have long to wait. A search party coming from another direction found the bodies of Imelda Riney and her son.

Sean Donnellan and his wife, Patsy, and Liam Pearl and his son started searching from a point northwest of where Fr Walsh's body had been found. They found the mother and child about a quarter of a mile north of where Fr Walsh had been found and much further into the forest.

Because of where the mother and child had been found it was easy to see why Brendan might not have found his way back there when he brought Fr Walsh to the forest. It would have been especially difficult to find this location at night.

22

Brendan's Story

JJ Muggivan

Brendan O'Donnell was questioned on several occasions throughout 7 May 1984. On one occasion, he told guards that the missing persons were 'okay'. 'Nobody will harm the child,' he said. Questioned later on in the day, he told the guards that he didn't 'give a fuck' about the missing persons, saying that nobody except his mother had ever cared about him, and that she was dead.

At another time, he said that he couldn't tell the guards anything. 'I don't want to talk about it,' he said, becoming upset. 'It's too late now. Leave it out. I'll not go into that.'

In the evening, when he was told that Fr Joseph Walsh's body had been found, and was asked about his involvement, Brendan said, 'You have his body and the forensic will do the rest.' He said that he didn't want to discuss it any further and that he couldn't tell the guards any more.

Brendan was asked if he accepted that the gun that had killed Fr Walsh had been in his possession, and he laughed at the guards, saying, 'You find that out. You're the fucking experts!'

He told the guards to keep searching in the wood for the other bodies. When asked to accompany the guards to Cregg Forest to show them the place where the other bodies were, Brendan complained that the 'fucking press' were all over the place and said that he would go only if there were no cameras.

He then began to speak about his experience in the Central Mental Hospital where he had had a friendship with John Gallagher from County Donegal, who had been found 'guilty but insane' of murdering his girlfriend and her mother in the grounds of Sligo General Hospital. Brendan told the guards that he had been going to 'do a John Gallagher' the night Fr Walsh's car was found burned out at Williamstown Pier.

A garda car left Loughrea barracks with Brendan hidden in the back seat to avoid the media. As the garda car drove towards Cregg Forest, a news report on the radio informed the occupants that the body of a woman had been found in a wood in County Clare.

Brendan shouted, 'You have it all now. We don't have to go any further.'

The guards asked where Liam's body was, and he said, 'You will find the child now. They're all shot.' He became upset and said he wanted to go to his mother's grave. 'Take me to my mother's grave,' he said. 'I know she's in heaven looking down at me. Why did I have to kill them? I'm worse than a fucking animal.'

He became increasingly agitated and shouted at the guards, 'Shoot me, you cunts. You haven't the balls.'

After a while, he calmed down and said that he no longer wanted to visit his mother's grave. 'Stop,' he said. 'Take me back. My mother won't want to see me now after all that I did. I've told you enough. I'm not showing you any more.'

On the return journey to Loughrea garda station, Brendan pointed out a shop where he had bought sardines and buns, and he showed the guards a wood where he had eaten them. He refused to discuss the deaths but told the guards about his father, and how he had not taken him back when he returned from England. He was more relaxed but still emotional.

The guards suggested that Brendan might like to see his father. At first, he declined, but then said that he would. He promised to tell the truth about the three deaths, saying that he would then be at peace with himself and would make peace with his father.

They arrived back in Loughrea and Brendan was returned to a cell. He met his father for a while and then made a statement, in which he said:

I will tell you what happened. I shot them all. I can't talk about it. I don't want to think about it. I must be evil. I had the gun for a while before that. I don't know what day I got it. You have the number and you know where I got it. I don't give a f . . .

The forensic will connect the gun. I will spend the rest of my life in jail. I don't give a f . . . I can do the time. I will go to Dundrum. At least I got the priest to pray for the woman and the youngster.

The priest said 'I don't mind dying.' Ye have my head screwed up. I'm not saying any more.

In an unsigned interview the following day, Brendan told the guards:

I had killing on my mind. I shot them from about 12 feet. The priest blessed them, the child had no pain, the woman went very white.

The blood poured out of the priest's head. The priest wasn't afraid to die. He said 'Don't shoot yourself, Brendan.' I got enjoyment out of it. The woman thought I was in the IRA. The Provos will get me for shooting the priest. I panicked. I couldn't bear to look at the child. I had to talk to somebody. My mind was gone till yesterday.

In another unsigned interview, he told the guards that he would be 'going down for 20 years'. He continued:

I deserve it. I should be shot. You should have given me lead today, it would be all over. Ye hadn't the fucking guts to do it, I can do my time. I have been in every prison in Ireland and a few in England. I was in Dundrum with Gallagher who shot the girlfriend in Sligo. He told me all about it. I bluffed the doctors that time. I will do it again.

He asked if he could see a priest, and arrangements were made for this.

* * *

Brendan went through three stages in his response to questioning about the killings: denial, cooperation, and confession. As his denial broke down, he showed remorse and acknowledgment of the evil of what he had done. After acknowledging the evil of his actions, he saw himself as having offended, initially at least, not God but his mother.

He did not remain too long without a plan for escaping the most severe penalty for his actions. When he realised he could no longer deny what he had done, he began thinking of the Central Mental Hospital, not prison. This plan dominated the next stage of his life. He was determined to escape prison.

His strategy for escaping prison and going to Dundrum took shape gradually. It began within hours of being caught. First he told guards:

I have been in every prison in Ireland and a few in England. I was in Dundrum with Gallagher who shot the girlfriend in Sligo. He told me all about it. I bluffed the doctors that time. I will do it again.

Later, he said:

I will spend the rest of my life in jail. I don't give a f . . ., I can do the time. I will go to Dundrum.

Brendan went on to talk about his experience in the Central Mental Hospital and about his friendship with John Gallagher, telling guards that he was going to 'do a John Gallagher' the night he had burned out Fr Walsh's car at Williamstown Pier. There had been some reports that John Gallagher had pretended to have attempted suicide by driving his car close to water and leaving it there.

On the previous Thursday night, Brendan had driven the priest's car onto rocks in Williamstown. The way the car had been left, burned out, it appeared as if he had attempted to drive it into deep water and drown himself. The location of the car was where his friend had drowned two years previously.

In a *Clare Champion* editorial a week after the arrest of Brendan O'Donnell, the editorial writer gave the opinion that the guards who had questioned Brendan believed that he had gone to Fr Walsh because of remorse at having killed Imelda Riney and Liam. The opinion was expressed that Fr Walsh had gone voluntarily with him to Cregg Forest in order to give the last rites to the dead mother and child. The opinion continued that something had gone wrong and Brendan had shot Fr Walsh.

The above opinion or theory is consistent with Brendan's state of mind after the bodies had been found. He was closer to telling the truth at that point than he was at his trial. By the time of the trial, he had developed a strategy to be sent to Dundrum Central Mental Hospital as opposed to Arbor Hill Prison.

23

Deteriorating Health

JJ Muggivan

In the twenty months before the trial, Brendan's mental and physical health deteriorated dramatically. He developed new and life-threatening illnesses. By the time of the trial, he probably was already terminally ill with only about eighteen months to live.

His new illnesses were brought about by a long hunger strike and psychotropic medication. None of these illnesses were identified by any of the experts who testified at his trial. Evidence of these new illnesses appeared in comments made by his defence lawyer, Mr Paddy MacEntee. Visitors who went to see Brendan in the twenty months prior to the trial were alarmed at his deterioration. They became more alarmed in the months after his trial until his death in July 1997. His visitors included Fr Neylon, Mary Quinn, Ann Marie, Tony Muggivan and Patrick MacEntee SC.

At the trial, Brendan's defence counsel, Patrick MacEntee SC, argued that the defendant was insane. He drew attention to Brendan's physical condition, brought on by the drugs he was taking. He described Brendan as being grossly overweight, with his tongue lolling to the side of his mouth, and his fingers stained with nicotine. He spoke of how Brendan had had dealings with mental-health professionals throughout his life from the age of about four.

It was reported that Brendan sat in the courtroom throughout, showing no reaction to anything that was said. A muscle in his jaw twitched and he ground his teeth. Later, he became fidgety and pulled at his moustache, bit his nails, tapped his foot and drummed his fingers on the wooden shelf in front of him. It is fairly clear from such reports that Brendan was in much distress from anti-psychotic medication at the time of his trial. He had become obese and a chain smoker.

It would seem that, at the time of the trial, he had been on the medicine for more than one year. He died a little over a year after the trial. In all, it seems that it took over two years for him to die from his medication.

Visitors were alarmed about Brendan's medicine from shortly after his imprisonment. Ann Marie and her grandmother saw him every couple of months. They had extreme trouble understanding what he was saying, whether on the phone or during a visit.

Brendan never discussed the murders with his sister or grandmother. Once, he said to them that they were shocking and should never have happened, but it was as if someone else had been responsible. His hands shook a lot, and Mary Quinn and Ann Marie felt that he was on heavy medication during the trial.

Brendan's visitors noticed that his memory seemed to be gone. On the phone, he would ask them when they were coming up, apparently thinking that they had not been there for a long time. Later, he gave up writing, calling or taking phone calls from his sister and grand-mother. Ann Marie complained on more than one occasion, but the staff told her that he would come out of it. Brendan phoned Tony about two months before he died. Tony had a lot of difficulty understanding Brendan as he was unable to talk. He promised to go to visit Brendan, but the visit never took place.

Mary Quinn recalled two men having to help her grandson to walk, as his head rolled from side to side. She said that she had never seen anything like it in her life and complained that he would not survive twenty-four hours if he did not receive medical care.

At the trial, Dr Charles Smith, Director of the Central Mental Hospital, testified that he had first seen Brendan in June 1988. Brendan was fourteen at the time and Dr Smith suspected that he was 'very close to psychosis, if not already there', and prescribed treatment for him. Brendan talked about powers, which Dr Smith did not regard as usual symptoms of schizophrenia, such as an ability to draw sparks. Dr Smith again saw Brendan in the Central Mental Hospital following his transfer from Spike Island. Dr Smith testified that self-injury, such as Brendan's to his left wrist, was quite common in people suffering from personality disorders. However, according to Dr Smith, in the three months that Brendan spent in Dundrum, there was 'no evidence to worry us about psychosis' and nothing to suggest psychiatric illness. They had diagnosed anti-social personality.

When Dr Smith saw Brendan on 14 May 1994, in the week following the discovery of the bodies of the missing people, he did not consider that Brendan was suffering from schizophrenia or a major mental illness. He and Dr Damian Mohan regarded him as very exited, animated and 'a disturbed young man'. He was almost an 'unmanageable prisoner'. They felt that Brendan might injure himself through aggression or frustration.

Dr Smith was unable to say what might have been going on in Brendan's head at the time of the killings. He believed that the defendant was suffering from a personality disorder, not schizophrenia, and said that people with personality disorders are usually held to be criminally responsible, as they do not have the interference experienced in schizophrenia.

According to Dr Smith, there was nothing about the case that would indicate a lack of criminal responsibility. He said that while psychosis fit with the concept of legal insanity, personality disorder did not.

Dr Smith, who had been a forensic psychiatrist for twenty-six years, gave the opinion that Brendan's trial hinged on the difference between psychosis and personality disorder. The latter was, he said, mainly a behavioural disorder, whereas in the former, behaviour was secondary to symptoms. He believed that Brendan suffered from a combination of an anti-social and borderline personality disorder. It was his view that Brendan had been feigning illness when, for some months in 1994, he had insisted on calling everybody Seamus. Later, in cross-examination by defence counsel Patrick MacEntee, Dr Smith agreed that he had been mistaken in saying that Brendan had ceased calling everybody Seamus when he had been returned for trial. However, he still maintained that Brendan had been doing it to mislead people into thinking he was insane.

In Dr Smith's opinion, it was possible that Brendan had had an organic psychotic episode. Staff at the Central Mental Hospital, believing his illness to be related to his self-imposed starvation and fluid deprivation, had organised for him to be sent back to Mountjoy Prison in

January 1995. Brendan had mutilated himself again and had been returned to Dundrum.

In Dr Smith's experience, it was rare for psychotic people to kill, and when they did, they were usually willing to admit to what they done.

When cross-examined by defence counsel Patrick MacEntee, Dr Smith agreed that at the age of fourteen, Brendan had been 'very close to psychosis if not already there'. He had prescribed anti-psychotic drugs for Brendan in 1988, and had assumed that his diagnosis was correct because Brendan's delusions had appeared to fade.

Mr MacEntee raised the issue of notes at the Central Mental Hospital in which psychiatrist Dr Gerry O'Neill had found Brendan to be 'normal'. Dr Smith agreed that these notes were inaccurate. However, he denied that they were 'a gross distortion'.

A note, dated 18 November 1994, was read in which Dr Art O'Conner had stated that Brendan wanted to die to get back to his mother. Brendan had been on a prolonged hunger strike in Mountjoy Prison and was admitted to the Central Mental Hospital that month. Dr O'Conner said in his note that there 'was an element of manipulation but [Brendan was] probably ill as well.' He had written that Brendan would probably be psychotic and depressed at times. He had therefore suggested an anti-psychotic drug and an anti-depressant.

Dr Smith testified that Brendan was being given Largactyl, an anti-psychotic drug, at that time. He said that his concern was to stimulate Brendan's appetite and he believed that the hunger strike had been decided on rationally.

Mr MacEntee produced a medical report from Mountjoy Prison, dated 29 May 1994, in which it was noted with regard to Brendan that there were 'no hallucinations now'.

Dr Smith agreed that this implied that there had been hallucinations between 9 May and 29 May 1994.

Dr Smith agreed with Mr MacEntee that the assessment of Brendan by Ballinasloe Mental Hospital had been 'far from ideal'. Mr MacEntee suggested that the hospital had had an obligation to discuss Brendan with Dr Kennedy, who had referred him there, and Ann Marie, who had had him committed. However, Dr Smith said that the diagnosis made by the staff at Ballinasloe did not differ from that which had been made at the Central Mental Hospital in 1990.

A medical note from Mountjoy Prison, dated 21 September 1994, stated that Brendan was 'medically fit for punishment'. Dr Smith said that in his view it was 'totally unprofessional to think in those terms'.

The next psychiatrist to give evidence was Dr Damian Mohan, who first saw Brendan on 9 May 1994, two days after his arrest. Between then and February 1995, he saw Brendan forty-two times.

Dr Mohan testified that when he interviewed Brendan on 9 May 1994, he saw no evidence of abnormality or defective reason, and that there was no evidence of schizophrenia or of depressive illness. Brendan told him that he had not been hearing voices, and apparently held no abnormal beliefs.

When Dr Mohan asked Brendan if he wished to die, the latter replied that he had 'nothing to lose'. 'A dog would have a better life than me,' he said.

Later, Dr Mohan had been concerned about Brendan's mental state and it had been reported that Brendan had told of the devil spiking his food and of being very lonely. According to Dr Mohan, on 7 September 1994, doctors interviewed Brendan from behind glass screen doors. When they asked about the deaths of Imelda and Liam

182

Riney and of Fr Walsh, Brendan replied that when he had been doing 'this', he had been 'fucked up'. He told them that he had been on 'a trip' at the time of the 'tragedy', and said, 'My head just went.' He asked the doctors, 'Why did I do it?'

Dr Mohan testified that in his dealings with Brendan, he had seen nothing that would have required in-patient treatment at the Central Mental Hospital.

From 4 July to 18 July 1994 and for other periods during his imprisonment, Brendan had been kept in a padded cell. Dr Mohan did not think that fourteen days was too long to keep someone in seclusion and said that he did not know how else the people in charge would have been able to handle him. On several occasions when Dr Mohan had seen him, Brendan had been dressed only in his under-pants. Dr Mohan said that he had not been aware that Brendan had defecated in the cell and had been seen sucking his thumb.

Dr Mohan agreed that drugs used to treat Margaret O'Donnell during her time in Ennis Psychiatric Hospital suggested that she had a psychiatric illness that might have been schizophrenia. However, when Mr MacEntee put it to him that Brendan was schizophrenic and that those doctors who said otherwise were affected by the determination not to have 'this troublesome patient' in the Central Mental Hospital, Dr Mohan replied that he had no vested interest in so doing.

Dr Brian McCaffrey, a consulting psychiatrist with the Eastern Health Board, had met Brendan in Mountjoy Prison in August 1994 at the request of the defence team. Brendan was handcuffed behind his back throughout the meeting and was accompanied by a prison officer, and there were other prison officers looking in at the door. Dr McCaffrey found the meeting unusual and very tense, and felt it to be a dangerous situation. He said that Brendan was 'very bizarre' and looked out of control.

Throughout the interview, Brendan called Dr McCaffrey Seamus, from which the doctor concluded that they were not on the same 'wavelength'. He asked Brendan who was in the government and Brendan said that he did not know. Albert Reynolds was Taoiseach at the time but when asked about him, Brendan responded, 'Does he make TVs?' He described Eamon de Valera as 'the best poet in Ireland'. Brendan's replies to questions were garbled and disjointed and he appeared not to be bothered at some level.

Dr McCaffrey testified that from this and subsequent meetings with Brendan, he formed the conclusion that he was 'quite psychotic' and suffering from a serious mental illness. He believed that Brendan had been suffering from a mental disease when he had shot Imelda Riney, and that he had been acting on commands from outside his mind. Dr McCaffrey said that he doubted that Brendan had known the nature or quality of his acts when he had shot his victims. While Brendan would have understood that he had a gun, that it was loaded and that a bullet came out, Dr McCaffrey was not sure that Brendan would have understood that a hit from the bullet would result in death. He said that Brendan seemed to have a blurred concept of death, citing as an example Margaret O'Donnell's funeral when her son had believed that she was smothered in her coffin and that he could save her.

It was Doctor McCaffrey's opinion that Brendan suffered from hebephrenic or disorganized schizophrenia at the time he killed his three victims and that he continued to suffer from this illness at the time of the trial. The illness would have rendered him incapable of understanding his actions. Dr McCaffrey told the court that he also believed Brendan to be psychotic.

Dr McCaffrey had interviewed Michael Pat O'Donnell in February 1995 and had found him to be friendly and cooperative. They had spoken about psychiatric illnesses experienced by Michael Pat's wife, mother and uncle. However, the doctor testified that he believed that Michael Pat O'Donnell had little insight into his son, whose material but not emotional needs were looked after by him.

According to Dr McCaffrey, when Brendan laughed when he talked of killing people, it was not an indication that he was feeling good. The fact of an outside expression not equating with an inner feeling was characteristic of schizophrenia, he said. He recalled that during his third interview with Brendan, in August 1994, Brendan had displayed a marked and obvious laugh and there had been big delays in his responses.

Dr McCaffrey testified that, on 11 November, he had noticed a big change in Brendan who was still in hospital. He had seen no signs of mental illness and no schizophrenia on this occasion.

In January 1995, Brendan was moved back to Mountjoy Prison where he cut his right wrist to the bone, through the tendons and arteries.

Dr McCaffrey testified that while Brendan could appear normal on occasion, he was actually very abnormal. He believed that the defendant was also exhibiting some features which might indicate a possibility of minimal brain damage, but said that this could not be established. It was his opinion that Brendan's schizophrenia had continued, with spikes of psychotic activity.

Dr Frances Knott, a clinical psychiatrist attached to the Eastern Health Board, also gave evidence at the trial. She expressed the view that Brendan was suffering from disorganized schizophrenia and was in a state of acute psychosis at the time of the killings.

Dr Knott testified that it was her belief that Brendan had been floridly psychotic when he was freed from prison in England in March 1994, and that he had remained in that state and would have been unable to control himself because of this. She explained that a person with hebephrenic schizophrenia was never well, although the severity of their symptoms might vary.

The doctor said that she was not surprised by the discrepancy between Brendan's statement that he had shot Fr Walsh twice in the head, and the pathologist's report that the priest had been shot once. Nor was she surprised by the fact that Brendan had not killed Imelda Riney in her house but had taken her to Cregg Wood. She believed that Brendan felt 'some magic' about the woods and that it had probably been 'a sort of ritual, bizarre killing'.

In his testimony at the trial, Dr Gerry O'Neill said that in laughing when he was describing the killing, Brendan had shown incongruous affect or emotion, which was very suggestive of schizophrenia. The doctor felt that while it was true that Brendan sometimes heard voices at apparently convenient times, such as when he was faced by a difficult question, he believed that schizophrenics could tell self-interested lies, as the disease does not absorb the whole personality.

When asked by the prosecution about the possibility that Brendan might, in fact, be suffering from a behavioural personality disorder, Dr O'Neill said that there were indications of both a personality disorder and schizophrenia.

Psychologist Dr Graham Turrall, for the defence, spoke in his testimony of Brendan's having chronic thought disorder and episodic disorganized schizophrenia. He testified that Brendan was suffering from a severe personality disorder which included avoidance, paranoia and an anti-social element.

The doctor described Brendan as an impulsive person who had difficulties with his identity. He believed that the killings had occurred because Brendan had been trying to control a situation in which he was not comfortable. He said that Brendan lied because he was trying to survive.

Dr Turrall referred to a doctor's note from 1988 in which there was a mention of 'the history of schizophrenia' in Margaret O'Donnell, and he said that that was the only reference he could find in Brendan's notes. He had also seen medical notes from jails in England where Brendan had been incarcerated from March 1993 to March 1994. These notes expressed concern about Brendan's mental state, and some mentioned bizarre behaviour and auditory hallucinations.

Fr Neylon, the former curate at Eyrecourt, also gave evidence. The priest had spent fifteen years in Eyrecourt and testified that Brendan had told him in 1992 of having slashed his wrist and been sent to the Central Mental Hospital. However, Fr Neylon was not aware that it was, in fact, another prisoner who had cut Brendan's wrist, at the request of the latter. Nor was he aware that Brendan had required microsurgery and had picked out the stitches with his teeth.

The priest testified that when he had asked Brendan if he knew that Fr Walsh was dead, Brendan had replied 'You must be joking. I know nothing about Fr Walsh. I know f . . . all. You must be raving.'

24

The Trial

JJ Muggivan

In his testimony, Brendan O'Donnell told the court that he had started a relationship with Imelda Riney in about April 1994. He said that although he was happy about this, he was 'very depressed' and hearing voices. He admitted that on the morning of Friday 29 April, he had broken into Edward Jameson's house. He said that when he had found no money there, he had taken a gun and a container of bullets, as he intended to rob Whitegate post office. He was hoping to get cash to go to France to live, and he told the court that Imelda was going to get him a passport.

Brendan testified that he walked across the fields to the house where Imelda was living. He said that he had the gun and ammunition with him and he fired at trees along the way. He said that when he arrived at the house at about 10.40 in the morning, he saw Imelda's car, but not the car of Val Ballance, her estranged husband. He went into the house.

According to Brendan, he met Imelda who was putting blue Wellington boots on her son. She questioned him about the gun and he told her that he had got it 'from Mr Jameson'. Brendan said that Imelda did not want the gun near her child, so he put it outside. He then returned inside, where Imelda put the kettle on to make tea.

Brendan's testimony was that he and Imelda then went upstairs and had sex, after which Liam Riney came up and made a remark. It should be noted that Imelda's family have always said that she would never have consented to sex with Brendan O'Donnell, and that she was not in a relationship with him. Mr MacEntee and Kevin Haugh SC, noting that semen was discovered in the body, stipulated that if the semen was examined it would be found to have been Brendan's. The examination of the body and the crime scene does not support a theory of violent rape occurring immediately prior to the killings. However, the absence of signs of a physically violent rape either at Imelda's house or at the crime scene does not justify a conclusion that what happened was not rape. Imelda Riney was not in a position at any time after meeting Brendan that morning to reject any demand or request made by him.

I believe that Brendan's testimony that 'Imelda put the kettle on to make tea' is, more or less, the starting point of embellishment and fabrication to persuade the jury of his insanity.

Brendan went on to tell the court that Imelda had just gone downstairs when:

I heard a voice from the devil telling me to kill Imelda, that she was the devil's daughter.

He said that he went down and told her that he would have to kill her because she was the devil's daughter, to which she replied, 'Don't be raving, Brendan.' He said that Imelda did not seem upset, so 'I went and got the gun and I pointed it at her and then she took me serious.'

Brendan then told Imelda to come with him. She was now holding Liam who was frightened. The gun was loaded. Brendan was asked how he was feeling at that point, and he replied, 'I don't know how to describe how I was feeling.'

Brendan got into the back of Imelda's car with Liam, and instructed Imelda to drive her car to Cregg Wood. He told the court, 'That's where I wanted to kill her. I decided to kill her when I heard the voice say she was the devil's daughter.'

Asked whether he and Imelda had talked during the drive, Brendan said that he could not remember. 'I was feeling very happy,' he said. 'Because I was going to kill the devil's daughter.' He said that Imelda was 'very nervous' when they got out of the car, but he could not remember if she had said anything. Liam was 'very nervous'.

'Me, I was happy,' Brendan told the court. 'I said, 'Imelda, lie down on the ground. I'm going to shoot you'.'

'She tried to pull the gun off me,' he continued. 'Imelda grabbed the barrel with her fists.'

Brendan's testimony went on:

> She pulled the gun. I pulled the trigger and I shot her in the eye and blood started squirting into the air.
>
> I wanted to kill her because she was the devil's daughter, because the devil told me to do it. I felt very happy, a lovely feeling.

According to the testimony Liam was sitting on the ground about 20 yards away and did not see when his mother was shot 'because of the trees'. He asked Brendan, 'Where's Mammy?'

Brendan told the court that he had been left without his own mother, and he did not want to leave Liam in the same situation. He brought the child over to his mother's body. 'I wanted them to be together,' he said. Unable to look at the child because of his 'innocent face', Brendan shot him in the side of the head.

At that point, according to Brendan, 'I felt happy he wasn't growing up without his mother.'

Brendan had been in court when Dr Charles Smith had testified against his insanity plea. Dr Smith had explained the necessity of 'voice commands from a psychotic disorder' in order to justify an insanity plea. Did Brendan pick up on this and supply the symptoms Dr Smith had said should be present in order to prove insanity?

The prosecution made the argument that Brendan had been stalking Imelda Riney throughout April 1994, and that he did not have any close contact with her until 29 April 1994. Under cross examination by Kevin Haugh SC, Brendan denied this, saying that he had known Imelda from 1991 or 1992. 'I wasn't watching her,' he said.

According to Brendan's testimony, following his release from prison in Wolverhampton in March 1994, he had spent three days in different parts of Ireland before returning to County Clare.

He said that he was familiar with Imelda's house as he himself had previously used it as a place to stay, and that IRA people on the run had also used it. He was surprised to find that it had been renovated and he visited about ten or twelve times before Val Ballance came on holiday in April 1994. He said that he continued to go there ever couple days and visited four or five times during Val Ballance's stay.

Brendan told the court that Oisín Riney attended Coolinbridge school. When informed by counsel that the school had been closed for repairs from 31 March to 19 April, Brendan replied that Imelda had told him that her son was at school. Counsel then told Brendan that Imelda's sister, Marie, had been staying with Imelda from 22 April, but Brendan denied this, saying that he had been at the house and that he had never seen her there.

According to Brendan's testimony, Imelda used to bring him a flask of tea and ham or salad sandwiches. Asked whether Imelda ate the ham sandwiches, he replied, 'She used to eat ham, yes.' However, Imelda was a strict vegetarian who did not herself eat meat, poultry or fish and would not have had ham in the house.

Prosecution counsel Kevin Haugh said to Brendan: 'You are deliberately lying and were never around Imelda Riney's house before April 29, 1994.'

Brendan replied, 'I'm not lying.'

In his testimony regarding the killing of Fr Joseph Walsh, Brendan told the court that he had eaten dinner at his grandmother's house on Tuesday 3 May and had left at about five o'clock. He said that the guards were looking for him about a robbery and the stabbing of his sister.

Brendan said that he slept that night in a hayshed near the village of Eyrecourt, and that when he was walking through the fields towards the village, he heard the devil's voice saying to him, 'Kill Father Joe. He's trying to christen the devil's son.' He did not know who the son was, but the christening was to be the following day.

It was raining, and Brendan waited outside Fr Walsh's house for about three hours. He managed to get halfway through the bathroom window but did not bother going inside.

Brendan said that he knew the priest 'fairly well'. When Fr Walsh arrived, Brendan told him to drive to Portumna. He said that he told the priest that he was going to kill him.

Fr Walsh drove Brendan to Cregg Wood but the gates were locked. They then proceeded to Cregg House. Brendan said that the priest told him 'that I was sick, that he knew my granny well and I shouldn't shoot him that he was not going to christen the devil's son.' He promised to give him money to go to England, but 'I said, "I'm going to kill you." I said, "You are trying to christen the devil's baby son and I'm gong to shoot you."'

Brendan testified that he and Fr Walsh stayed in Cregg House until seven o'clock the following morning. He smiled as he said that the birds were singing at that time. He told the court that the priest gave him thirty pounds and a valuable gold watch that had been a present from his sister. According to Brendan, Fr Walsh told him that he could sell the watch.

Fr Walsh drove back to Cregg Wood with Brendan. The curate said that he would withdraw money for Brendan from the bank in Banagher and asked to be let go. When they arrived at a clearing in the forest, Brendan told the priest to kneel down, so that he would not fall and 'get hurt'. Fr Walsh said to him, 'If you shoot me, will you see that I'm buried in the diocese I served in?' Asked what his reply to this had been, Brendan said, 'I said I wouldn't because he was trying to christen the devil's baby son.' Brendan testified that the priest knelt down and 'I shot him in the head.'

Fr Walsh went into convulsions, Brendan said, so he shot him again in the back of the head 'so he wouldn't go through any pain'.

Brendan told the court that he 'felt happy after' the killing. 'I had killed a man who was trying to christen the devil's baby son,' he said.

Laughing, Brendan testified that after he had shot Fr Walsh, the priest's 'brains came out'. Brendan then 'felt happy' as he drove to Limerick

On his arrival in Limerick, Brendan had a meal at a restaurant but vomited in the street afterwards. He said that he saw people in Limerick laughing at him. He drove around for a few days after that.

Asked what the devil looked like, Brendan said, 'He is about 8 feet tall, and he has evil green cat's eyes, and he has hooves — not feet — and he smokes a pipe.'

25

The Defence

JJ Muggivan

In his closing argument, Brendan O'Donnell's defence counsel, Patrick MacEntee SC, drew the attention of the jury to the fact that one of the doctors involved in the commitment of Brendan O'Donnell to Ballinasloe Mental Hospital had expressed the view that Brendan was schizophrenic. However, the hospital had discharged him two weeks later, having made a provisional diagnosis of personality disorder or paranoid ideation.

Counsel pointed out that this provisional diagnosis had been made in late 1992, which was approximately a year and a half before the events of April and May 1994.

Brendan had been administered the drug Triptasol at the age of four and Largactyl at the age of fourteen. Counsel argued that as a schoolboy, Brendan was already showing signs of developing schizophrenia.

Patrick MacEntee argued that at the time of the killings, Brendan was suffering from hebephrenic or disorganized schizophrenia. This had caused him not to know the nature or quality of his acts. He said that his client did not know his actions were wrong and, even if he did know, his mental illness would have prevented him from stopping himself from committing them.

Brendan's defence counsel urged the jury to find insanity as Brendan's motivation in committing the killings. He pointed to his client's physical condition as he sat in court, and described his life of contact with mental-health professionals, from the age of four. After he had been discharged from Ballinasloe Mental Hospital, Brendan had gone to Britain where he had reportedly been arrested in Edinburgh in March 1993, in relation to a theft that had occurred two years previously. By the time he returned to Ireland a year later, Brendan had been in three young offenders' institutions and two hospitals. His defence counsel recounted Ann Marie's description of Brendan O'Donnell telling her on 26 April 1994 of having hazy eyes and of seeing things in front of his eyes.

Patrick MacEntee described Brendan's actions of the following days as not being the actions of a sane man. He emphasised that his client had apparently taken Imelda Riney from her home in broad daylight in her car which was familiar to the people of the area. Brendan had burnt Imelda Riney's car and had also driven around for a while in Fr Walsh's car before burning it too.

According to the defence counsel, the action of openly carrying around a gun while there was a major garda search was not indicative of the actions of a sane man. The action of placing Liam Riney's body beside that of his mother was also interpreted by counsel as a curious act — an act of returning the child to his mother.

Patrick MacEntee attributed Fiona Sampson's survival of her ordeal to her intuitive knowledge of how to deal with a lunatic. He argued that there was no evidence that his client took pleasure in killing. He suggested that while Brendan did tell shallow, silly lies, he did not tell the lies of a cold, calculating and sane killer. He pointed to the testimony of three psychiatrists who had given the opinion that Brendan suffered from schizophrenia and the testimony of all of the doctors, whether for the state or the defence, who had stated that schizophrenia was a major mental illness

Did Patrick MacEntee come close to identifying Brendan O'Donnell's most serious health problems when he pointed out that his client was grossly overweight from drugs, with his tongue lolling to the side of his mouth, and his fingers coated with nicotine?

Did non-mental-health professionals, such as Patrick MacEntee SC, Mary Quinn, Ann Marie O'Donnell and Fr Neylon come close to describing diseases identified by Dr Peter Breggin in his book, *Toxic Psychiatry*?

In his book, Dr Breggin suggests that drugs such as those which Brendan was taking, rather than treating a disease, can actually create it. He writes that 'the drug reaction can get completely out of hand' and that the result can be a disease that is similar to a type of encephalitis. Such a disease would have symptoms including 'lobotomy-like indifference', fever, sweating and heart problems. In severe cases, those affected could become delirious, fall into a coma and die.

Some affected people might apparently make a complete recovery only to slip suddenly backwards months or even years later. Some might develop Parkinson's, while others might become psychotic or develop dementia, symptoms of which might include 'silliness, erratic moods, difficulty focusing attention, wandering speech, disconnected thoughts, talking too directly in the listener's face . . . .'

Dr Breggin writes:

> The profession of psychiatry now agrees that the drug-induced neurological disorders do become permanent in a large percentage of patients. In addition, there is growing incontrovertible evidence that permanent psychosis and dementia also are frequent outcomes. (Breggin, *Toxic Psychiatry*)

If the patient ceases to take the medication, the nervous system cannot cope and there may be psychotic symptoms and even greater anxiety and anguish. Therefore, patients who are trying to come off such drugs require emotional and social support, and professional supervision.

There is a risk that withdrawal symptoms may develop, and these could range 'from insomnia and hyperactivity to hallucinations and delusions'. Moreover, the patient will still ultimately be left having to deal with their original emotional problems.

Dr Breggin writes that, 'for the control of unwanted behavior', medication is often given to children in institutional care, including 'facilities for delinquents'. Children treated with drugs such as those with which Brendan was treated may become fidgety and very anxious, thus requiring ever larger doses of their medication which was originally prescribed to deal with those very symptoms.

The psychiatric care Brendan received was criticised at the end of the trial, and the then Minister for Health, Michael Noonan, ordered an inquiry into how psychiatric services had dealt with him. The inquiry was never carried out.

Brendan O'Donnell's painful experience was not yet over, though.

26

The Verdict and Aftermath

JJ Muggivan

---

ccording to news reports, the jury in the Brendan O'Donnell trial returned to the court about two hours after commencing deliberations, requesting the transcript of several medical witnesses and the testimony of Ann Marie O'Donnell. The reports did not identify which medical testimony the jury wished to review. Ann Marie O'Donnell's factual testimony was very supportive of the expert testimony suggesting that Brendan O'Donnell had been hallucinating for some time, was schizophrenic, was paranoid, and was not capable of acting rationally. The judge acknowledged the difficulties experienced by the jury in the light of such a lengthy trial, but explained that it was not possible to grant their request.

The fact that the jury requested these parts of the transcript suggests a desire to pay close attention to the legal standards for determining insanity in the case of Brendan O'Donnell. The verdict that was finally reached was that Brendan O'Donnell did not meet the legal standard for insanity.

Brendan O'Donnell was found guilty of the murders and initially sentenced to life in prison. A short time later, he was given an additional four life sentences.

At the time of his trial, Brendan was already dying from his medication.

Shortly after being sentenced, Brendan was transferred to Dundrum by Dr Charles Smith. Dr Smith, in his deposition given for the inquest, acknowledged that Brendan was a very troubled young man, and stated that he had agreed that although he had not been found to be insane, Brendan could stay in Dundrum after his trial, until such time as he settled clinically. Brendan had been transferred from Mountjoy to Dundrum prior to the trial because of his hunger and thirst strike, and had started to eat and drink shortly afterwards.

After the trial, Brendan was transferred to Arbor Hill, but by arrangement with the Governor at that prison, he was moved back to Dundrum.

However, according to Dr Smith, Brendan never really settled into a comfortable routine, and remained in the admission unit of the Central Mental Hospital. Dr Smith said that Brendan 'presented regularly with bizarre physical symptoms for which we could find no explanation'. During this time, he was prescribed various medications, though never in high dosage. According to Dr Smith, nothing that was prescribed for Brendan seemed to be particularly beneficial.

At the end of May 1997, Mary Quinn and her granddaughter visited Brendan. They said that he was 'not too bad that day'. He was 'a bit fidgety' but not as bad as he had been previously, and he spent time talking to his nephew, Aaron.

The staff at Dundrum were still concerned about the threat posed by Brendan but believed that he was actually most likely to harm himself. Some time after this visit, he broke a window with his fist and was sent to St Vincent's Hospital where he was treated for lacerations.

On 22 July 1997, in order to tranquillise him after this incident, Brendan O'Donnell was given 100mg of a drug called Thoridazine, and the following day he had 200mg of it. On 24 July, Brendan was found dead.

Ann Marie had spent the previous day with her grand-mother, because it was her birthday. She returned to Portumna that night. On the evening of 22 July, she was ironing when Brendan 'came straight into my head, for no reason at all'. The following morning, her son came to her bedroom door to tell her that there was a guard looking for her.

The guard told Ann Marie that her brother had passed away either late the previous night or early that morning. He told her that Brendan had died of natural causes. The guards had heard the report on the radio first, and had then had a phone call from Dr Smith in the Central Mental Hospital.

Ann Marie went to the garda station from where she spoke by phone with Dr Smith. The doctor told her 'that he was very sorry for what had happened. A guard who was with Ann Marie prompted her to ask Dr Smith whether her brother had been on medication. The doctor said that he had been and explained about Brendan's having hurt his hand. He said that the staff in Dundrum had performed CPR on Brendan when they had found him that morning, but when there was no response, they realised that he was dead.

Ann Marie was told that her brother's body was on its way to the coroner's, and would not be available to the family for a few days. The following morning, she agreed that Brendan's remains would be cremated.

On 26 November 1997, Ann Marie and her grandmother attended the inquest into Brendan's death. They listened as Dr Charles Smith spoke of Brendan's self-mutilation, and described him as 'one of the most complicated, problematic patients I have ever dealt with'. He said that Brendan's had been a life with very little pleasure or achievement and one in which he was constantly challenging and fighting those in authority. Ultimately this had led to Brendan's becoming extremely dangerous, destroying the lives of his victims and destroying his own chances of achieving any degree of contentment.

According to Ann Marie, Dr Smith 'didn't see anything wrong with the amount of medicine he got and [said] that he would have had a problem believing that the medicine killed him, that he believed it was cardiac arrest.'

Dr Smith gave evidence that other inmates had received the same amounts of medication, without the same result.

However, according to Ann Marie, the state pathologist, Dr John Harbison, was of the opinion that 'Brendan O'Donnell died of overdosage of the drug Thioridazine'.

Ann Marie and her grandmother had to leave for a bus. The inquest jury put Brendan's death down to misadventure. Michael Pat O'Donnell wanted to know only where and when his son had died.

On 30 June 1998, my brother, Tony Muggivan, visited Ann Marie and gave her the money needed to purchase a copy of the coroner's report on her brother's death. Ann Marie O'Donnell requested the report on her brother's death, and paid the fee. Several months later, she obtained a copy.

According to a Department of Justice report, a year and a half after his death, Brendan was 'being prescribed powerful, mood altering drugs when he died at the age of 21 in the custody of the Central Mental Hospital'. As the State does not keep records of prisoners' prescriptions, it was impossible to know in what amounts these drugs were being administered. The same report revealed that the cost spent on drugs for prisoners in Ireland was almost three times the amount per person outside the prison system, and more than four times the cost per prisoner in English jails.

Brendan O'Donnell's experience of institutional mental-health care confirms in dramatic detail what Dr Peter Breggin has written about such institutions elsewhere in the world.

27

An Injured Brain

JJ Muggivan

The state pathologist's post-mortem report noted 'considerable venous pressure' and 'tiny areas of bleeding' in Brendan's brain. The brain was retained for possible further examination later.

Dr Harbison suggested that Brendan's brain was at the lower limit of normal for size and weight, weighing 1,195g. However, according to Henry Gray, author of *Gray's Anatomy*, it would seem that the size of the brain is not a very important issue.

What is more important, however, is evidence, or lack of evidence, of shrinkage. If there was shrinkage, it could have come from early use of Valium and later use of anti-psychotic medication. Signs of damage or injury in the frontal lobe area would also be significant.

Dr Harbison's report found physical evidence that Brendan had extensive brain injury.

> The upper surface appeared slightly flattened, due to fixation without sufficient buoyancy or suspension. Two small areas of prominent veins with possible small leakage of blood were present on the convex surface of the left frontal lobe and a third on the left occipital lobe, none of these more than 5mm wide or 10mm long.
> (RECORD OF VERDICT, 26 November 1997)

Dr Graham Turrall, a clinical psychologist practising in Toronto, Canada, gave evidence that Brendan had had 'considerable difficulties' with psychological tests, which had judged him to have a mental age well below his actual age. According to Dr Turrall, 'Other tests were suggestive of brain dysfunction in the frontal lobe area.'

Researchers into brain function have written about cases where patients laugh or giggle for no apparent reason. For example, in their book, *Phantoms in the Brain*, V.S. Ramachandran and Sandra Blakeslee cite an account of a fifteen-year-old girl who was being treated surgically for epilepsy. The girl was awake for the procedure, and laughed uncontrollably when certain parts of her brain were stimulated in the course of the operation.

They also write of a neurological disorder in which patients do not register pain:

> Patients with this condition do not register pain when they are deliberately jabbed in the finger with a sharp needle. Instead of saying, 'ouch!' they say, 'Doctor, I can feel the pain but it doesn't hurt' . . . many of them actually start giggling, as if they were being tickled and not stabbed. . . .

The authors explain that this syndrome is often seen in cases of damage to a specific part of the brain that normally registers pain and sends messages regarding the agony of pain. They describe the result:

> One part of the person's brain (the insular cortex) tells him, 'Here is something painful, a potential threat,' while another part (the cingulate gyrus of the limbic system) says a fraction of a second later, 'Oh, don't worry; this is no threat at all.'

From early childhood, Brendan had episodes of unusual laughter, silliness, and giggling. It was seen by his parents who reported it to Dr Ledwith. It was also seen by his sister, by my brother, Tony, and his family, by Kevin Brennan at Trinity House, by the Monaghans, by his grandmother, and by doctors who treated him.

More than one psychiatrist referred during their testimony at his trial to Brendan's unusual laughing. However, they appeared to treat it as something to be expected with a disorder such as schizophrenia. Dr Peter Breggin, however, identifies unusual laughing as a clear sign of brain injury. With Brendan, it was a lifelong behaviour, suggesting that the brain injury giving rise to it occurred early.

Post Traumatic Stress Disorder (PTSD) can be caused by 'witnessing an event that involves death, injury, or a threat to the physical integrity of another person.' The person witnessing the event will experience 'intense fear, help-lessness, or horror (or in children, the response must involve disorganized or agitated behaviour. . . .)' (DSM-IV-TR, p. 463)

When Brendan was brought to see Dr Ledwith initially, Margaret O'Donnell told the doctor that her son's usual reaction to stress or tension was to freeze and turn pale. As far as we know, this behaviour was reported after Brendan had witnessed his mother's suicide attempt. He experienced at least two events which might have caused Post-Traumatic Stress Disorder, namely his mother's attempted suicide and her death and burial.

Research in the US has found that Vietnam veterans with very severe PTSD suffered brain shrinkage of about 25 per cent. Their performance in verbal memory tests was about 40 per cent below that of others of comparable age and education. The researchers discovered that:

> PTSD patients' difficulties with putting feelings into words are mirrored in actual changes in brain activity. (Bessel A. Van der Kolk, Alexander C. McFarlane, and Lars Weisaeth, eds, *Traumatic Stress*, p. 233)

Those suffering from severe PTSD can also experience 'auditory hallucinations and paranoid ideation' (DSM-IV-TR, p. 465).

Valium consumed by a mother has a direct effect on the foetus. It is capable of causing physical addiction in the foetus and withdrawal symptoms at birth. Children born with an addiction to alcohol often have damage to the frontal lobes of their brain, and the effects of Valium addiction are similar to those of addiction to alcohol. The frontal lobes of the brain 'control judgement, inhibition, concentration, self-control, conscience, personality and emotional traits as well as cognition and memory, motor speech and movement skills' (Fetal Alcohol Syndrome Link).

Brendan first reported fear of his food when he told his mother that he saw animals in it. He was about five years old at the time. The record reports that he was given medicine to improve his appetite.

He seems to have had a lifelong paranoia about being in danger from food, and his first dangerous assault resulted from his belief that his sister was trying to poison him.

This kind of fear can be debilitating and may have been at the root of his attempted suicide by starvation prior to his trial. It seems that he was given medication again for his appetite.

Credible new research suggests that fear of food or disgust with food involves precise nerve cells in very specific subregions of the brain. Brendan's fear of food may have started from hallucinations caused by addiction to Valium.

The following is a list of symptoms reported during Brendan O'Donnell's childhood:

- Higher than normal to dangerously high pain tolerance (See above discussion on laughing)
- Severe loss of intellectual functioning
- Behavioural problems
- Attention deficit disorder
- Extreme impulsiveness
- Poor judgement
- Little or no capacity for moral judgement
- Little or no capacity for interpersonal empathy
- Sociopathic behaviour
- Developmental delay
- Sleep disorder
- Night terrors
- Social problems
- Depression
- Reactive outbursts
- Suicide
- Death.

The above can all be associated with neurological damage in children. All have been identified as problems experienced by children who have been exposed to high levels of alcohol while still in the womb. The effects of a drug such as Valium would be similar.

From early on, Brendan was reported as having symptoms such as clinging, shadowing, not sleeping in his own bed, and wanting to sleep with his mother. Such symptoms are typical of Separation Anxiety Disorder, and in Brendan's case seem to have been precipitated by a combination of medicine reactions and an over-protective mother. It has been found that this disorder 'is relatively more frequent in children of mothers with Panic Disorder' (DSM-IV-TR).

Those suffering from Separation Anxiety Disorder will become excessively anxious on being separated from the home or from those to whom they have become attached, and will tend to 'cling to' or 'shadow' a parent. They may also be reluctant to attend school.

A child such as Brendan O'Donnell can put enormous stress on a parent and can evoke harsh treatment. When parents of such children engage in excessive discipline, it needs to be understood that they are attempting to have their child become a child who performs like other children.

Of all of the possible causes for Brendan O'Donnell's difficulties, parental discipline seems to be the least likely cause of his major problems. His ability to learn the normal rules for living and his ability to cooperate with authority were severely impaired from infancy.

However, research has shown that the response of parents is important to such a child. Aggression on the part of a parent will lead to counter-aggression in a child.

Brendan's parents were in conflict, and so were incapable of providing consistent limits for him. He learned complex manipulative skills by exploiting parental disagreement over how to handle him. Margaret became more protective and Michael Pat may have become more critical.

Traumatised children in particular put enormous stress on family members and on those who have to live with them and teach them. It is also true that parents in serious personal emotional distress put enormous stress on their spouses and children.

Margaret O'Donnell, because of her illnesses, was a source of distress for her mother, her siblings, her husband, and her children. She traumatised Brendan by attempting suicide in his presence. She very likely injured him with her consumption of medication while she was pregnant.

As Brendan's symptoms worsened, he, in turn, increased the stress on all members of his family.

A suicidal mother can traumatise an entire family just as much as an abusive husband can with physical violence. Serious illness necessitating constant attention and medication can sustain a high state of distress for partner and children alike.

Not being able to give relief to such an individual can cause guilt, shame, hopelessness, depression, and, ultimately, anger in all family members.

As the youngest child for nine years, Brendan seems to have borne the brunt of his mother's distress. He seems to have taken on the responsibility for taking care of her. He experienced the ultimate failure when she died when he was nine years old. He was never able to let go of the memory of his mother and her unhappy life.

Conclusion

JJ Muggivan

W hen Tony and I first embarked on the task of telling Brendan O'Donnell's story, we assumed that we already knew the story and that all we had to do was write it. Little did we know then how much more we were going to discover. Years later, we are continuing to make discoveries. We are sure our account is not the last word on how and why he came to behave the way he did, but we hope that we have added substantially to what is already known about what motivated him.

As I look back on our account of his life, I have found myself asking questions only touched on so far. There is one question that has always been in the back of my mind: how did Brendan feel as he heard the story of his life recounted during his trial? In other words, what kind of sense did he make of what he heard about himself?

He listened day after day to details of his life. He heard accounts of how he had reported worms coming out of his ears when he was a young child, of seeing animals in his food, and of how he feared being harmed or poisoned by germs. He heard about how he could not sleep alone because of monsters in his room and how he was afraid to go to school. He heard about his early problems with aggression, wetting his bed at night and wetting his pants during the day, and his strange habit of laughing when in distress or pain. He heard about his strange tendency to become rigid and turn pale when under stress.

He listened to accounts of his mother's depression, her need for large amounts of medication, her unhappy marriage, and her trips to doctors and hospitals. He heard of how she was always in distress, depressed, or wanting to die. He heard about his mother's attempts at suicide, her death, and her burial. He heard of how he was restrained when he tried to jump into her grave to stop the burial, thinking she was being buried alive.

He could see the looks and glances directed at him in the courtroom. He could hear the gasps of horror as testimony of his violent actions was presented. As the story of his life unfolded in front of him, he recognised most of what he heard. The story was familiar to him: it was his life.

He heard the gardaí describe his response to the news of the discovery of the first body, how he screamed that he must be worse than an animal, and that his mother could never forgive him now. He listened as they described his remorse and guilt.

He was unable to make sense of what his life was about and it is unlikely that what he heard helped him. He had given up on understanding why he was the way he was and he no longer expected anyone to help him. The best he could hope for from the proceedings was assignment to the Central Mental Hospital in Dundrum, as opposed to Arbor Hill Prison.

Throughout the proceedings, Brendan learned very little about what disorder or disorders he suffered from. However, he learned criteria for a successful insanity plea, or at least enough to help him make an attempt to manipulate the jury into sending him to a hospital rather than a prison.

Ironically, his attempt to manipulate the jury is revealing about both his symptoms and how he learned to use them. I am concentrating on two particular symptoms to demonstrate how Brendan was capable of rationally using serious health symptoms to achieve a purpose. The two symptoms I discuss here are his fear of being poisoned and his unusual laughter at times when he should have been manifesting distress or pain. These two symptoms were evident early in his life and persisted until they were suppressed by the powerful anti-psychotic medicine he was administered in the months before his trial and death.

Not long after he was imprisoned, Brendan stopped eating. He claimed he was on hunger strike and gave political reasons for not eating, such as claiming he was a member of the IRA. He lost an alarming amount of weight and, reportedly, was at risk of dying from starvation. I believe his 'hunger strike' was caused by a new upsurge of his life-long paranoia about being poisoned by something in his food. However, he was able to use rationally what resulted from paranoia as a protest against his imprisonment and as a ploy to be hospitalised. He was prescribed large amounts of anti-psychotic medicine to help him with his appetite and force him off his hunger strike. Meanwhile, his paranoid belief about being poisoned continued to go undetected. Most likely, the anti-psychotic medicine helped him with his appetite because it relieved his paranoia. The medication suppressed his paranoid fear of food so effectively that he became obese in the following months. In fact, the medication even suppressed his fear of cigarettes. He had never smoked before in his life, but in the months of imprisonment prior to his trial, he became a chain smoker. Brendan's strategy had worked. Because of his 'hunger strike' he had been transferred from prison to hospital.

The second example of Brendan using a symptom strategically to achieve a rational purpose was his use of his unusual laughter. When he was called to testify, he wanted to impress the jury that he met the insanity standard. He had become familiar with this standard from talking to experts and, in particular, from listening to Dr Smith's testimony. Dr Smith catalogued the symptoms required for an insanity verdict and testified that Brendan did not have those symptoms.

Having heard the criteria for an insanity plea, Brendan used his life-long symptoms of unusual laughter and hallucinations to embellish his account of how and why he killed his victims. He was exploiting what the jury had heard about his laughter by giving an account of how he 'enjoyed' doing the 'devil's work'. He described how he laughed at what he was doing when he was killing his victims, how he heard the devil issue commands and how he followed these commands because he enjoyed doing what the devil ordered. In this way, Brendan was attempting to meet the criminal insanity standard laid out by Dr Smith, namely, the need to hear hallucinatory commands to perform the wrongful actions. It seems that this was a spontaneous embellishment produced by Brendan as he sat in court. He may even have surprised his own experts, as well as his barrister. He certainly surprised everyone when he described what the devil looked like in his hallucinations.

These two examples of Brendan's mental-health symptoms, and how he used them to manipulate, demonstrate what can be deceptive features of paranoid delusional disorder. On the one hand, an individual can have a very serious and dangerous mental-health disorder, and on the other, he can appear rational and symptom-free.

Brendan always knew that he was different. He knew that there was something seriously wrong with him. He was always baffled by the way his brain functioned. He didn't know why he lived with such fear, anxiety and paranoia. He didn't know why he heard voices when there was no one there. He didn't know why he had a strange laugh. He didn't know why he feared food or how this fear started. In short, he didn't know why his brain played tricks on him.

Few understood that he was living in the prison of his injured brain. Those who were close to him knew there was something seriously wrong but didn't have the resources to help him.

Now, we may be able to connect his symptoms to what produced them. This was something Brendan could never do. When he presented his symptoms to experts, they were not understood as symptoms of a serious — and dangerous — mental-health disorder. The best he could do with his symptoms was exploit them to escape prison in order to go to a hospital for the criminally insane. When he did this, he heard himself described as a cunning person, attempting to avoid the consequences of his wrongdoing. He was described as 'bad, not mad'. In reality, his ability to exploit his symptoms was a result of his life-long familiarity with his own strangeness.

He was the ultimate fugitive, running from his fears and demons. What he was running from was within him. He was unable to give his demons form or identity; thus he was unable to fight them. He produced fantasy enemies as a way of externalising his inner world of fear and terror. He created dangerous situations and practised strategies for self-preservation and survival. This caused him to spend his life in readiness for danger and attack. His life was dedicated to preparing for fight or flight — the ultimate survival instincts. In times of intense fear and paranoia, he was capable of destroying anyone or anything he imagined might stand in the way of his survival.

When Tony and I talked at the beginning of the telling of this story, we were determined not to produce an account of a 'mystery'. We agreed that producing an account of a 'mystery' would not be worth the effort required. We hope that if others re-examine this story for more insight and more knowledge, they will also have this aspiration. We need to continue our efforts to understand young people like Brendan so that we can give the necessary help in time. Shrouding a story like this in mystery and intrigue might be entertaining but, in the final analysis, gaining knowledge and insight is what counts.

We tried to keep the focus on Brendan O'Donnell. We tried not to focus on the victims or their families. We did not wish to cause any additional pain. We know that any reminder of what was suffered by the victims will cause their families pain. We hope that we have been sensitive. We believe that what we have uncovered about Brendan will help us to recognise young people like him before they can inflict such pain on themselves, their families, and, above all, on their potential victims.

Index

Index

219

221